The Best in Children's Nonfiction

The Best in Children's Nonfiction

Reading, Writing, and Teaching
Orbis Pictus Award Books

Edited by

Myra Zarnowski
Queens College, City University of New York

Richard M. Kerper
Millersville University

Julie M. Jensen
The University of Texas at Austin

National Council of Teachers of English
1111 W. Kenyon Road, Urbana, Illinois 61801-1096

Illustration from AN EXTRAORDINARY LIFE by Laurence Pringle. Copyright © 1997 by Laurence Pringle. Published by Orchard Books, a division of Scholastic Inc. Reprinted by permission of Scholastic Inc.

Illustration from MINN OF THE MISSISSIPPI by Holling Clancy Holling. Copyright © 1951 by Holling Clancy Holling. Reprinted by permission of Houghton Mifflin Company. All rights reserved.

Staff Editor: Bonny Graham

Interior Design: Doug Burnett

Cover Design: Evelyn C. Shapiro

NCTE Stock Number: 04894-3050

Library of Congress Cataloging-in-Publication Data

The best in children's nonfiction : reading, writing, and teaching Orbis Pictus Award books / edited by Myra Zarnowski, Richard M. Kerper, Julie M. Jensen.
    p. cm.
   Includes bibliographical references.
   ISBN 0-8141-0489-4
   1. Orbis Pictus Award. 2. Children's literature, American—History and criticism. 3. Children's literature, American—Bibliography. I. Zarnowski, Myra, 1945– II. Kerper, Richard M. III. Jensen, Julie M.

Z1037.A2 B47 2001
028.1'62—dc21
                        2001044261

Contents

Introduction

Several years ago, the members of the Orbis Pictus Award for Outstanding Nonfiction for Children Committee decided that it would be a good idea to do more than select award-winning titles. We wanted to tell people about the ideas that excited and infuriated us about recent nonfiction, about the insights we were developing about the genre as we read healthy doses of it over the years, and about our "noticings" about the radical and subtle changes occurring in the literature.

As discussion about this book continued, we realized that in addition to hearing from committee members, readers would enjoy hearing from writers whose books have been selected by the committee. We then invited several authors to look back on their careers during the past decade as they wrote nonfiction for children.

Finally, we decided that a complete listing of all Orbis Pictus winners, honor books, and recommended titles for the past ten years would be a handy reference for teachers and school librarians. Therefore, we have provided annotations for all winners and honor books and a complete listing of recommended titles for the first decade of the award, 1990–1999. Because the 2000 award winners had been announced by the time this book was in production, in an appendix to the 1990–1999 bibliography we have reprinted the Talking about Books section of *Language Arts* that features the 2000 award winner and honor books.

The Best in Children's Nonfiction, then, is organized in three parts: Section I, in which committee members discuss the characteristics of good nonfiction; Section II, perspectives on nonfiction and writing nonfiction from authors of award-winning titles; and Section III, a complete listing of Orbis Pictus titles for the last decade, including annotations of award-winning and honor books.

Serving on the Orbis Pictus Award Committee has truly enriched my life as a reader. I know I speak for the committee in inviting you to share the riches.

Myra Zarnowski

1 Ten Years of the Orbis Pictus Award

Edited by Myra Zarnowski

The Orbis Pictus Award for Outstanding Nonfiction for Children was established in 1989 to promote and recognize excellence in nonfiction writing for children. The award's name commemorates Johannes Amos Comenius's (1657) work *Orbis Pictus (The World in Pictures)*, considered to be the first book actually intended for children. Each year one award book and up to five honor books are named. In addition, the award committee selects other titles it considers to be outstanding. Selecting Orbis Pictus Award–winning titles is a big job. Committee members sift and sort through hundreds of books looking for the very best in nonfiction. What's surprising is how, at the end of each year, there is a high level of consensus about which books we want to honor.

Before we reach this consensus, we talk, talk, and talk some more. During our committee meetings, members bring and brag about their favorite titles. You might hear comments such as: "Have you *seen* this book? Isn't it great? I tried it with third graders and they just loved it." Or you might hear, "This is exactly the kind of book we need!" But then, you also might hear us voice our concerns: "Is the information in this book worth knowing? Is it important enough to spend time on?" Or, "Would this book be useful in the classroom? Would children understand it? Is it really *for* children?"

In this section, current and past members of the Orbis Pictus Award Committee share our thoughts about issues that have sparked our discussions over the years. First, Julie Jensen discusses the quality of writing found in award-winning titles. She shows how good nonfiction writers have applied the tools of storytellers to information they have gathered through extensive research in order to write the kind of prose we want to read again and again. In Chapter 2, Myra Zarnowski discusses the intermingling of fact and fiction that has been occurring with greater and greater frequency within the genre marketed and sold as nonfiction. Noting that this is part of a larger trend in both children's and adult nonfiction, she suggests other methods—short of fictionalizing—that writers have developed for dealing with information that does not fit neatly within a story framework. Then Richard Kerper considers the changes in book design that correspond to advances in digital technology. He discusses the historical roots of these newer digital features that allow us to point-and-click with our eyes, as well as other current innovations in nonfiction book design. In Chapter 4, Karen Patricia Smith explains why careful documentation of sources is an essential component of nonfiction for children. Using examples drawn from Orbis Pictus Award–winning books, she shows how documentation is much more than citing and labeling. Finally, Elaine Aoki examines the criterion of significance as a means of evaluating quality nonfiction. She discusses how a book's impact, its relation-ship to current concerns, and its wide applicability to curricula influence the committee's selection process.

Together, the essays in this section highlight current issues and trends in nonfiction for children. These same issues and trends appear again in Section II, where nonfiction authors discuss their work, and in Section III, where committee members annotate and discuss award-winning titles.

The Quality of Prose in Orbis Pictus Award Books

Julie M. Jensen
The University of Texas at Austin

Ten years ago when the National Council of Teachers of English (NCTE) established the Orbis Pictus Award, Sylvia Vardell (1991) built a case for celebrating nonfiction, described the new award, and outlined four features of outstanding books. Winning authors were to meet criteria related to (1) accuracy, (2) organization, (3) design, and (4) style. Authors were to use rich language and appropriate terminology; they were to write in an interesting and stimulating way; their enthusiasm for the subject matter was to be evident; and they were to encourage children's curiosity and wonder.

After emphasizing style as "the distinctive voice of the author that reaches out to an audience with irresistible conviction" (1991, p. 475), Vardell wrote, "The best of the genre (just like the best fiction for children) offers an outstanding model of quality of writing, individuality of style, beauty of expression, and creativity in the use of language" (p. 475). Finally, she contended that in matters of style, "the evaluation of fiction and nonfiction may be surprisingly similar. For an informational book must be interesting and well-written, use rich and vivid language, reflect the author's unique voice and passion, and involve and stimulate the reader, just as a good work of fiction should" (p. 478).

Writing style in a nonfiction book for children should be, as in all literature, a work of art. Artful prose engages the reader; offers information and enjoyment; is imaginative, accurate, thought provoking, and memorable; and is born of meticulous research.

The Foundation of Style in Award-Winning Nonfiction

Award-winning prose floats on mastery of subject matter, mastery that comes from research both wide and deep. While it may be possible to ruin good information with bad writing, even good writing cannot overcome bad information. Winning authors have taken to heart the axiom "write what you know"; their writing reflects a recognition that reliable information is the sine qua non of good writing. Reports of authors investing more time on research than on drafting, revising, and editing their prose are commonplace.

Clearly, authors of Orbis Pictus Award–winning titles are thorough researchers. How else would they find the authentic dialogue, the pithy quotes, the fascinating anecdotes? How else would they transform their curiosity about a topic into a heartfelt passion for it? How else would they discover possible links between a topic and children's interests? Research uncovers both what a child *might like* to know and what a child *should* know; it provides choice among details, quotes, and anecdotes that might capture a child's interest in language accessible to that child. Facklam (1999), in an apt metaphor, describes her research as a whole bowl of spaghetti in which she searches for the strand that is her story.

But research does not end with finding that narrative strand. As soon as they begin to write, authors often discover that their narrative has taken them into areas they do not adequately know or understand, with the consequence that, even as their manuscripts are going to press, winning authors may still be searching for additional information to enrich or lend accuracy to their prose. Laurence Pringle (1986), recognizing the potential influence of his books on readers, never risks breaking the reader-writer bond by allowing a possible error to creep into his prose. And Jim Murphy, in an interview with Yoder (1999), says that responsible writers use experts to check for missing information or to discuss specific aspects of a subject: "Never sit back and say, 'I know everything there is to know about this subject.' Next remember that people . . . can differ a great deal about what they consider the truth. I try to get two or more verifications for all details in my books, and to present a balanced view of opinions, too" (p. 280).

For Russell Freedman (1992), research that leads to thinking with clarity leads, in turn, to writing with clarity. Hard, specific facts enliven language; both major and minute details illuminate an event, a place, or a personality. Revealing his process, Freedman says:

> Starting a new book is always like trying to solve a puzzle. You have to decide what to include and what to leave out, how to begin, what to emphasize, how much, and where, how to balance facts and interpretation, and how to breathe life into the subject. The process of viewing the material, of seeing what belongs where, is a mystery I never resolve once and for all. I spend a lot of time looking for revealing details, for meaningful anecdotes and quotations that will help bring my factual material to life. (p. 8)

Milton Meltzer (1993), a historian who writes about real men and women facing the social issues of their time, describes his process in comparable fashion:

In preparing to write such a history I read as widely as possible in the available sources, both primary and secondary, making notes on what I think I may want to use. At the same time I hunt everywhere for the documentary material that will let people speak in their own words. I don't mean only the kings and generals—the Lords of Creation—I mean the anonymous ones upon whom society rests and without whom the superstructure would collapse. Their words are found in letters, journals, diaries, autobiographies, in songs and poems, in speeches, in court testimony and in legislative hearings, in newspaper reports, in eyewitness accounts, and, more recently, in oral history interviews. I want the reader to discover how it felt to be alive at that time, I want the reader to share directly in that experience, to know the doubts, the hopes, the fears, the anger and the joy of the men, women, and children who were the blood and bone of that history. (p. 28)

As these writers attest, scholarly research makes possible both the concrete and the more elusive elements of style. Winning books draw readers in by developing vivid, elaborate, readily visualized scenes; they breathe life into characters through personal details found in quotes from diaries and letters; they use enlightening, sometimes humorous, anecdotes that hold interest and reveal character. They maintain an artistic vision of the larger context by attending to its specifics. We learn about the Dust Bowl through intimate knowledge of one school in *Children of the Dust Bowl: The True Story of the School at Weedpatch Camp* (Stanley, 1992); we learn about the catastrophic Chicago fire through the eyes of four observers in *The Great Fire* (Murphy, 1995); we learn about the life cycle of the monarch butterfly from one such butterfly named Daneus in *An Extraordinary Life* (Pringle, 1997); and we learn about the history of the American West from a train trip made by Robert Louis Stevenson in *Across America on an Emigrant Train* (Murphy, 1993).

On Defining Style

If, in fact, "It's all in the telling," then how an author writes, or *style*, is an all-important criterion for judging nonfiction. Critics of the eleven Orbis Pictus Award–winning titles use recurring descriptors of the prose styles found in these books: "lively," "readable," "inviting," "engaging," "lyrical," "dramatic," "vivid." Yet, in concrete and precise terms, what is it about their style that merits adjectives such as these?

In *On Writing Well* (1998), Zinsser says,

the secret of good writing is to strip every sentence to its cleanest components. Every word that serves no function, every long word that could be a short word, every adverb that carries the same meaning that's already in the verb, every passive construction that leaves the reader unsure of who is doing what—these are the thousand and one adulterants that weaken the strength of a sentence. (pp. 7–8)

In total concurrence are Strunk and White, in this familiar paragraph from *The Elements of Style* (1979):

Vigorous writing is concise. A sentence should contain no unnecessary words, a paragraph no unnecessary sentences, for the same reason that a drawing should have no unnecessary lines and a machine no unnecessary parts. This requires not that the writer make all his sentences short, or that he avoid all detail and treat his subjects only in outline, but that every word tell. (p. 23)

Still, although definitions of good writing may parallel each other, they fail to fully satisfy. Many writers on writing acknowledge a certain mystery about style, a feeling that talking about it means leaving solid ground. For example, Strunk and White concede, "There is no satisfactory explanation of style, no infallible guide to good writing" (1979, p. 66), and they go on to conclude that "style takes its final shape more from attitudes of mind than from principles of composition" (p. 84).

Writers of nonfiction for children have joined the effort to both define and stress literary merit. For example, Milton Meltzer urges critics to look at literary style:

What literary distinction, if any, does the book have? And here I do not mean the striking choice of word or image but the personal style revealed. I ask whether the writer's personal voice is heard in the book. In the writer who cares, there is a pressure of feeling which emerges in the rhythm of the sentences, in the choice of details, in the color of the language. Style in this sense is not a trick of rhetoric or a decorative daub; it is a quality of vision. It cannot be separated from the author's character because the tone of voice in which the book is written expresses how a human being thinks and feels. If the writer is indifferent, bored, stupid, or mechanical, it will show in the work. (1976, pp. 21–22)

If style is important, and satisfying explanations of it are elusive, possibilities for demonstrating it abound. For example, here is prose described as "completely convincing," "exciting," and "dramatic." It is Robert Burleigh's spare lead from his 1991 award-winning *Flight: The Journey of Charles Lindbergh*:

It is 1927, and his name is Charles Lindbergh.
Later they will call him the Lone Eagle.
Later they will call him Lucky Lindy.
But not now.

> Now it is May 20, 1927, and he is standing in the still-dark dawn. He watches the rain drizzle down on the airfield. And on his small airplane. The airplane has a name painted on its side: *Spirit of St. Louis.* (unpaged)

Having fulfilled the purpose of a strong lead—grabbing the reader's attention—Burleigh continues to entice readers to join him on Lindbergh's suspenseful thirty-three-and-a-half-hour flight:

> He has five chicken sandwiches with him. That is all the food he has brought. But he eats nothing. It's easier to stay awake on an empty stomach. His body cries for sleep. He loses track of time. The night is endless. (unpaged)

This writing has been stripped to its cleanest components (Zinsser, 1998); it is concise—every word tells; it reflects the "attitudes of mind" of its author (Strunk & White, 1979); and the reader hears Burleigh's unmistakable voice in the rhythm of the sentences, the drama-enhancing details, and the color of the language (Meltzer, 1976). Each Orbis Pictus Award–winning author has a particular way of using language. Each has found a distinctive voice, a method of sharing information, a pattern for organizing experience—in short, a unique style.

Narrative Style in Award-Winning Books

Reviewers have made it clear that readers can come to Orbis Pictus Award books not only in search of trustworthy information but also to discover a compelling story. Some reviewers' comments include:

Children of the Dust Bowl: The True Story of the School at Weedpatch Camp, Jerry Stanley (1992)
"The story is inspiring, and Stanley has recorded the details with passion and dignity."
    Booklist, September 1992

Across America on an Emigrant Train, Jim Murphy (1993)
"Using the narrative thread of Stevenson's journey, author Jim Murphy weaves in a great deal of information about the historical context."
    Language Arts, October 1994

The Great Fire, Jim Murphy (1995)
". . . reads like a too-good-to-put-down novel."
    Language Arts, October 1996

An Extraordinary Life: The Story of a Monarch Butterfly (Pringle, 1997)
"Combines the craft of the fiction writer with the non-fiction writer's attention to accuracy."
    Language Arts, November 1998

Nonfiction titles reviewed by Orbis Pictus committees reflect diverse formats—picture books, chapter books, photo-essays, interviews, journals, activity books, reference works, handbooks—and multiple approaches to sharing facts, ideas, and concepts. Authors arrange and connect ideas in ways typically associated with expository style (describing, temporal sequencing, explaining, comparing/contrasting, defining and giving examples, identifying problems/solutions), but the lines between exposition and narration are clearly blurred. Rosenblatt (1991) observes, "narrative (story) is found not only in novels but also in scientific accounts of geological change or historical accounts of political events or social life" (p. 444). Though information in nonfiction may or may not be integrated within the framework of a story, it is clear from the review excerpts opening this section that authors of winning titles enlivened their nonfiction through the artistic use of narrative techniques traditionally associated with fiction.

None of the ten winning titles is a textbookish or encyclopedic collection of mind-numbing facts. In each, information is woven into a compelling narrative framework, one that is interesting and consequential to young readers. Content is selected and shaped in a way that engages readers from page one and inspires them to explore further, to experience a sense of wonder, to read the book again and again. Using the tools of storytellers, authors create living, breathing characters; settings that transport the reader in time and place; gripping action; and a significant unifying focus. These authors are masters of the word picture, of the anecdote, of authentic dialogue, of fascinating detail. On the artful use of storytelling techniques, two of the winners, Russell Freedman and Jean Fritz, speak for themselves:

> I think of myself first of all as a storyteller, and I do my best to give dramatic shape to my subject, whatever it is. I always feel that I have a story to tell that is worth telling, and I want to tell it as clearly, as simply, and as forcefully as I can. By storytelling, I do not mean making things up, of course. . . . As a writer of nonfiction, I have a pact with the reader to stick to the facts. . . . [But] facts in a literal sense do not rule out art or imagination. . . . There's a story to almost everything, and the task of the nonfiction writer is to find the story—the narrative line—that exists in nearly every subject. (Freedman, 1993, p. 42)

> Nonfiction can be told in a narrative voice and still maintain its integrity. . . . The art of fiction is making up facts; the art of nonfiction is using facts to make up a form. (Fritz, 1988, p. 759)

How are narrative elements reflected in the ten winning titles? Jean Fritz, widely regarded as a master of the nonfiction genre, was the first Orbis Pictus Award winner. James Madison is just one of the historical figures she has brought to life through authentic detail, humor, anecdote, a visual setting, and a balanced portrayal of her subject's strengths and weaknesses. She begins *The Great Little Madison* by focusing on an unexpected element—Madison's voice—and thereby captures her reader:

> James Madison was a small, pale, sickly boy with a weak voice. If he tried to shout, the shout shriveled up in his throat, but of course he was still young. His voice might grow old as he did. Or he might never need a big voice. (1989, p. 1)

Like Fritz, Russell Freedman is widely praised for biographies of historical figures, among them Eleanor Roosevelt, Orville and Wilbur Wright, and Abraham Lincoln. Akin to his other books, the Orbis Pictus–winning *Franklin Delano Roosevelt* (1990) blends Roosevelt's private and public lives, his shortcomings and achievements, into a detailed, lively, and stimulating narrative, one filled with anecdotes and quotes by and about FDR. In *Flight* (1991), excerpted earlier, Robert Burleigh uses Charles Lindbergh's journal to develop his character and setting, a plane so sparely equipped that it allows no forward vision. Through printed sources and personal interviews, Jerry Stanley's *Children of the Dust Bowl* (1992) creates a portrait of Leo Hart, an inspired and inspiring educator readers won't forget. But larger than Hart is a well-crafted and engrossing social history of the Great Depression. Jim Murphy's *Across America on an Emigrant Train* (1993) informs readers about the development of the American West and informs writers about the development of setting and character. Following is an excerpt from the journal of Murphy's subject, Robert Louis Stevenson:

> When the train crossed a metal bridge spanning a wide river, Stevenson leaned over the platform railing to ask the brakeman sitting on the roof the river's name. The brakeman shouted back, "The Susquehanna River."
> [Stevenson writes in his journal,] "The beauty of the name seemed to be a part of the beauty of the land. . . . There is no part of the world where [the names are] so rich, poetical, humorous, and picturesque as the United States of America. All times, races, and languages have brought their contributions. . . . The names of the States and Territories themselves form a chorus of sweet and most romantic vocables: Delaware, Ohio, Indiana, Florida, Dakota, Iowa, Wyoming, Minnesota, and the Carolinas; there are few poems with nobler music to the ear; a songful, tuneful land." (p. 43)

In *Safari beneath the Sea* (1994), Diane Swanson lures her readers into an unusual conflict—that among flowerlike, brightly colored, finger-length sea animals called anemones:

When one colony grows toward another, war may break out. The anemones beat each other using tiny clubs packed with stinging cells. Unless one of the colonies draws back, the anemones fight to the death. In the end, what is left between them is a bare strip of rock—a peace zone—that neither colony can enter without starting another war. (pp. 22–24)

Published accounts, personal letters, journals, and other original sources enabled Jim Murphy to construct (and deconstruct) Chicago through the eyes of four individuals who witnessed *The Great Fire* (1995) of 1871. And using da Vinci's own writings and the words of those who responded to him and his work, Diane Stanley creates a lively and informative portrait of *Leonardo da Vinci* (1996). In a deft paragraph on da Vinci's extensive notebooks, Stanley encapsulates the multifaceted genius of her subject:

Over the years he filled thousands of pages with the outpourings of his amazing mind. There were drawings of grotesque faces, drafts of letters, sketches for future paintings, lists of books he owned, plans for inventions, moral observations, pages copied out of books he had borrowed, notes of things to remember, designs for weapons, drawings of anatomy, and observations of nature. On one page, for example, you can find geometry problems, a plan for building canals, and the note "Tuesday: bread, meat, wine, fruit, vegetables, salad." (unpaged)

From the sights and sounds of a rural New England evening, *An Extraordinary Life* (1997) follows a single monarch butterfly on an obstacle-laden journey to Mexico. Listen to the sounds of nature in Laurence Pringle's lead for his scrupulously researched and enticing story:

It was a moonless night in late August. Field crickets chirped in a Massachusetts hayfield. Their chorus was joined by tree crickets, and by katydids from the forest edge. The lush life of summer would soon be over, and the night-calling insects chirped and trilled insistently. They were engaged in the serious business of attracting mates and producing the next generation—the musicians that would play in the evening concerts of next summer. (p. 1)

Finally, *Shipwreck at the Bottom of the World* (1998) has the beginning, middle, and end, and the drama, the actions, and the characters, of a fine novel. Jennifer Armstrong uses anecdotes and dialogue from journals to develop the courageous and loyal character of Sir Ernest Shackleton and to chill her readers with the harshness of life in the Antarctic:

In the winter, the temperature can sink to 100 degrees below zero Fahrenheit. Cold air masses sliding down the sides of the glaciers speed up until they become winds of close to 200 miles per hour.

When winter descends on the southern continent, the seas surrounding the land begin to freeze at the terrifying rate of two square miles every minute, until the frozen sea reaches an area of 7 million square miles, about twice the size of the United States. It is truly the most hostile environment this side of the moon. Just imagine yourself stranded in such a place.

In 1915, a British crew of twenty-eight men *was* stranded there, with no ship and no way to contact the outside world. They all survived. (p. 1)

Matisse is said to have concluded: "There's nothing more difficult for a truly creative painter than to paint a rose, because before he can do so, he has first to forget all the roses that were ever painted." Orbis Pictus Award–winning authors approached topics that had been written about before: Antarctic exploration, flying the Atlantic, Franklin Delano Roosevelt, James Madison, the American West, the burning of Chicago, monarch butterflies, Leonardo da Vinci, the Dust Bowl era, and life undersea. They began with composition skills, techniques of exposition and narration, research data, "attitudes of mind," and more. They ended with ten stylistically unique creations that engage, inform, give pleasure, and are worthy of the Orbis Pictus Award. "It's all in the telling."

References

Facklam, M. (1999). From research to the printed page. Paper presented at Highlights Foundation Writers Workshop, Chautauqua, NY.

Freedman, R. (1992). Fact or fiction? In E.V. Freeman & D.G. Person, (Eds.), *Using nonfiction trade books in the elementary classroom: From ants to zeppelins* (pp. 2–10). Urbana, IL: National Council of Teachers of English.

Freedman, R. (1993). Bring 'em back alive. In M. O. Tunnell & R. Ammon (Eds.), *The story of ourselves* (pp. 41–47). Portsmouth, NH: Heinemann.

Fritz, J. (1988). Biography: Readability plus responsibility. *The Horn Book, 64,* 759–60.

Meltzer, M. (1976). Where do all the prizes go? The case for nonfiction. *The Horn Book, 52,* 21–22.

Meltzer, M. (1993). Voices from the past. In M.O. Tunnell & R. Ammon (Eds.), *The story of ourselves: Teaching history through children's literature* (pp. 27–32). Portsmouth, NH: Heinemann.

Pringle, L. (1986). Science writing. Paper presented at Highlights Foundation Writers Workshop, Chautauqua, NY.

Rosenblatt, L. M. (1991). Literature—S.O.S.! *Language Arts, 68,* 444–48.

Strunk, Jr. W., & White, E. B. (1979). *The elements of style* (3rd ed.). New York: Macmillan.

Vardell, S. (1991). A new 'picture of the world': The NCTE Orbis Pictus Award for outstanding nonfiction for children. *Language Arts, 68,* 474–79.

Yoder, C. (1999). Tales of a revolutionary voyage. In S. Tierney, (Ed.), *Children's writer guide* (pp. 271–82). West Redding, CT: Institute of Children's Literature.

Zinsser, W. (1998). *On writing well* (6th ed.). New York: HarperColllins.

Children's Books

Armstrong, J. (1998). *Shipwreck at the bottom of the world: The extraordinary true story of Shackleton and the* Endurance. New York: Crown.

Burleigh, R. (1991). *Flight: The journey of Charles Lindbergh.* New York: Philomel Books.

Freedman, R. (1990). *Franklin Delano Roosevelt.* New York: Clarion Books.

Fritz, J. (1989). *The great little Madison.* New York: G. P. Putnam's Sons.

Murphy, J. (1993). *Across America on an emigrant train.* New York: Clarion Books.

Murphy, J. (1995). *The great fire.* New York: Scholastic.

Pringle, L. (1997). *An extraordinary life: The story of a monarch butterfly.* Illus. B. Marstall. New York: Orchard Books.

Stanley, D. (1996). *Leonardo da Vinci.* New York: Morrow Junior Books.

Stanley, J. (1992). *Children of the dust bowl: The true story of the school at Weedpatch Camp.* New York: Crown.

Swanson, D. (1994). *Safari beneath the sea: The wonder world of the north Pacific coast.* San Francisco: Sierra Club Books for Children.

Intermingling Fact and Fiction

Myra Zarnowski
Queens College, City University of New York

When a girl touring the White House is yanked into a painting hanging on the wall and given her own personal tour by none other than George Washington (Harness, 1998), or when civil rights activists both living and dead confront each other on a talking bus (Ringgold, 1999), or when newly minted letters masquerading as historical documents are mixed in with the actual stuff of history (Peacock, 1998), here we have clear-cut examples of fictionalization in children's books. Whatever the reasons for this phenomenon—to engage readers on an emotional level, to tell a "better" story than the straight facts might allow, or to fill in the empty spaces in what is currently known—this trend is steadily growing. In an article in the *Journal of Children's Literature*, book reviewers Miriam Martinez and Marcia Nash refer to fictionalizing as "a *stylistic option* increasingly used by authors of informational books" (1998, p.12; emphasis added).

Although it is clear that fictionalization is a presence to be contended with, for members of the Orbis Pictus Award Committee it is not considered a stylistic option. Quite frankly, the Orbis Pictus Award Committee has had many soul-searching conversations on this topic, and many of these conversations involve our own winning choices. For example, when Laurence Pringle, author of *An Extraordinary Life: The Story of a Monarch Butterfly* (1997), the 1998 Orbis Pictus Award winner, introduced us to what was to become the main focus of his book—a single monarch butterfly—by telling us, "Let's call this caterpillar, the one that emerged from her mother's last egg, Danaus" (p. 13), we were surprised; we were really stumped, though, when we read later on that Danaus, now a butterfly, narrowly escaped being eaten by an oriole by letting go of her perch on a tree, and that "from that day on she rested in the lower parts of trees, where orioles and grosbeaks rarely hunted" (p. 48). Was this a thinking butterfly who learned from her experience? Or was this merely standard, smart butterfly behavior? Ultimately, through conversations with the author and with other scientists, we were convinced that the latter was true. The following year, when reading Jennifer Armstrong's gripping account *Shipwreck at the Bottom of the World: The Extraordinary True Story of Shackleton and the* Endurance (1998), a book that would become the 1999 Orbis Pictus Award winner, committee members wondered about the dialogue reported to have taken place among the various crew members on the ship. In reporting this dialogue, the author drew on the writings of Sir Ernest Shackleton, the leader of this famous Antarctic expedition; Leonard Hussey, the expedition's meteorologist; Frank Worsley, the ship's captain; and Harry McNeish, the ship's carpenter; and on photos by Frank Hurley, the expedition photographer. Yet we could not always tell which work was the source of the dialogue reported. Sometimes we even wondered how the men had managed to record such extensive dialogue given the life-threatening hardships they were enduring. So while we wished for clearer documentation, we were at the same time impressed by the author's extensive research. Armstrong spent time at the Scott Polar Research Institute in Cambridge, England, where she consulted with experts and was given access to archival material and library holdings. She also included an extensive bibliography. In the end, we decided to trust this extensive research.

The 1998 Orbis Pictus honor book *Kennedy Assassinated! The World Mourns: A Reporter's Story* (1997), Wilborn Hampton's page-turning account of how he happened to cover the presidential assassination, raised similar questions for us. While we were gripped by the unique perspective offered by an eyewitness reporter to an event he referred to as "the biggest story of my life" (p. 89), we wondered how the author could recall extensive amounts of dialogue from that day in 1963 when confusion was swirling around him. These reading experiences bring to mind Joyce Carol Oates's comment about believing what she reads: "'Interesting—if true' is a skeptic phrase that has imprinted itself permanently on my consciousness" (Oates, 1998, p. A24). Like Oates, Orbis Pictus committee members tend to read children's nonfiction with a "prove-it-to-me" stance.

This should not be surprising given that the intermingling of fact and fiction in children's books is only a part of a larger trend in literature—children's and adult—to incorporate greater and greater amounts of fiction into what is marketed as nonfiction. One account of mixing fact and fiction in adult literature can serve as a representative example of this larger trend. In an article that appeared in the *New York Times* entitled "Now! Read the True (More or Less) Story!" (Carvajal, 1998), it was reported that John Berendt, author of the bestselling nonfiction title *Midnight in the Garden of Good and Evil,* had not only created dialogue attributed to real life people, but he had also invented scenes within the story itself. According to Berendt, "I call it rounding the corners to make a better narrative. . . . This is not hard-nosed reporting because clearly I made it up" (E1). Defending this approach, he stated, "The truth that I was telling was the actual story, and I do not think that I distorted the truth by cutting these corners. . . . It was entertainment; it was show biz. . . . They're getting the same story, and they're getting it better" (E4). Not everyone agrees. Nonfiction writer H. G. Bissinger, quoted in the same article, put it this way: "Maybe I'm old-fashioned, but what makes nonfiction great is that a reader is getting something based on the truth." He said he "felt 'robbed' by the fictional smoothing of *Midnight.*"

Writers and critics of children's nonfiction have voiced similar concerns about "rounding the corners" in children's books. Penny Colman, author of several outstanding works of nonfiction including *Rosie the Riveter,* a 1996 Orbis Pictus honor book, stated in a recent issue of *The New Advocate,* "Needless to say, I reject the trend in recent years in which some writers add fiction to their nonfiction books in order to move the story along or to make it more dramatic or to introduce facts" (Colman, 1999, p. 217). She suggests calling these "blended books" by some new title, perhaps "informational fiction." Julie Cummins, in an article in *School Library Journal,* coined the term *storyographies* to describe the outpouring of fictionalized picture book biographies with created dialogue and fictional characters. These books, she explains, provide "a 'story presentation' rather than a factual recounting" (Cummins, 1998, p. 42). Cummins raises the relevant question, "How far can the story stray from the facts?" (p. 43). For nonfiction writers such as Penny Colman and Russell Freedman, the answer is *not at all*. In a recent commentary entitled "On Telling the Truth" (1998), Freedman reminds us that imaginary scenes and invented dialogue, once the stock-in-trade of biographies for children, are no longer acceptable. Instead, he provides another route for engaging young readers: "Nowadays, a nonfiction children's book demands unwavering focus and the most artful use of language and storytelling techniques" (p. 225). But these techniques are secondary to the need to tell the truth. According to Freedman, "Writers can only interpret the truth as they hear it. They are answerable in that interpretation to their readers, with whom they have an unwritten but clearly understood pact to be as factually accurate as human frailty will allow" (p. 225).

Another idea that frequently emerges during discussions of fictionalizing is that fiction somehow provides us with a "higher truth" that can be achieved only when writers are not constrained by facts. This has been referred to as "a creative truth," as opposed to "a historical truth" (Marc Norman, quoted in Sterngold, 1998, B9), or being "truthful rather than factual" (Joseph Mitchell, quoted in Yagoda, 1998, p. 6). But what does this mean? Is this the seamless story that seems so satisfying and so marketable? Is this history or science without boredom? Or is it simply anti-intellectual?

For a long time educators assumed that for children learning to read, narrative was primary, and that only later did they come to understand informational text. It has also been suggested that fictionalized texts are needed "to engage student interest" (Leal, 1995, p. 199). Yet an ever growing body of evidence shows us that this is not so. A recent article in *Language Arts* (Caswell & Duke, 1998) describes how for some children—in this case, children having difficulty learning to read—nonfiction is a "way in" to literacy, a way that capitalizes on children's background knowledge and genuine interests. But this will occur only if we see knowledge seeking as motivational (Alexander, 1997), as answering our deepest needs to know about the past, the present, and the possibilities for the future.

To be fair, it is also important to recognize that there are several strong proponents of intermingling fiction and nonfiction. Recent advocates such as Jenkins (1999) point to the success of the Magic School Bus series and emphasize that the final pages of each book unravel and clarify the fact/fiction mix within the text. Pappas, Kiefer, and Levstik (1999) claim that "fuzzy" texts—those that mix storybook and information book genres—are not necessarily less coherent or comprehensible or of lesser quality. These advocates of fictionalized text would clearly be in favor of stretching the boundaries of what we call nonfiction, while others would like to see these books categorized as something else.

Innovations in Nonfiction: Filling in the Gaps While Avoiding the "Stretchers"

Nonfiction writers have developed several innovative techniques for dealing with information that does not fit neatly into a story framework. Some innovations are ways of dealing with gaps in existing information that might prevent a writer from telling a well-rounded story. Others are ways of dealing with the range of possible interpretations of the known facts, but again, in ways that move beyond the story framework. Four of these authoring techniques are discussed in the following paragraphs as possible options to fictionalizing: (1) admit it, (2) provide competing theories, (3) create a plausible scenario, *but* be sure the reader knows that you are doing it, and (4) use a nonstory format. Each of these techniques allows the writer to deal with what is known without stretching the truth.

1. Admit It. Sometimes when there are gaps in available information, nonfiction authors simply admit it. There are a number of instances of this, particularly in history books. Authors writing about William Shakespeare, for example, must deal with the lack of information about his personal life. In *Bard of Avon* (1992), authors Diane Stanley and Peter Vennema admit in an author's note that "much of his life is a mystery to us" (unpaged). As a result, their writing is often tentative. They identify missing information with phrases such as "we don't know," "no one knows," or "it does not appear." At other times, the authors speculate using hedging terms such as "perhaps," "it is quite possible," or "probably." A recent book by Aliki, *William Shakespeare & the Globe* (1999), also refers to Shakespeare as a mystery, highlights the lack of personal information about him, and discusses the need to study the times in which he lived and guess at the rest.

Admitting when evidence does not exist frees the biographer to look at what does exist that might shed light on the subject—a study of the times in which the person lived, what others have said about the person, and the creative works the person left behind. It also provokes informed conjecture—how things might have been.

"Admitting it" frees the science writer, too, from the need to have a definite, decisive ending. In *The Snake Scientist* (1999), author Sy Montgomery ends her fascinating description of the work of zoologist Bob Mason with a list of unanswered questions Mason and his colleagues plan to work on in the future. Books that use "admit it" as a writing technique provide a model for young writers of how to deal with the unanswered aspects of their own research.

2. Provide Competing Hypotheses or Scenarios. When authors are not sure how something happened and there are several competing hypotheses, one way to deal with the situation is to present all of the hypotheses and discuss their merits and flaws. In *Dinosaur Ghosts: The Mystery of Coelophysis* (1997), author J. Lynett Gillette uses this strategy. After explaining the position in which certain dinosaur skeletons were found—some nearly complete and others disjointed—she discusses several theories about what happened to them. Were they stuck in the mud? Caught in an erupting volcano? Poisoned by water? Each hypothesis is evaluated in turn until the author presents what she considers "our best idea" (p. 30).

Historians also can present competing scenarios. In *What's the Deal? Jefferson, Napoleon, and the Louisiana Purchase* (1998), author Rhoda Blumberg discusses the fact that the Louisiana Purchase was not inevitable, but rather the result of Napoleon Bonaparte's conscious decision to sell. If he had kept Louisiana, Blumberg suggests, the territory might have (1) grown strong enough to challenge the United States, (2) been conquered by the British, or (3) been conquered by the United States in alliance with England. Other likely scenarios are presented as well. Similarly, in *The Mary Celeste: An Unsolved Mystery from History* (Yolen & Stemple, 1999), readers are introduced to six theories of what happened to a ship found adrift at sea in 1872 with her entire crew missing. Readers are challenged to think about what happened to them and determine which theory makes the best sense.

Providing competing hypotheses or scenarios is a technique that introduces young readers to how scientists and historians think about the evidence they encounter. It unmasks the uncertainties they must deal with and provides a glimpse into the process of sifting and shaping information. If readers learn this type of thinking early, they will know from the start that neither science nor history is about amassing an archive of facts, but instead about thinking about the facts, asking new questions, and trying to discover new answers.

3. Create a Plausible Scenario, *But* Be Sure the Reader Knows You Are Doing It. When it isn't possible to know exactly what happened but there is evidence from which to surmise, writers can use that information to build a plausible scenario. The reader, however, must be clearly alerted to this case building. One excellent example of this strategy can be found in *Discovering the Iceman* (1996) by Shelley Tanaka. In "Part One: The Discovery," the author first explains how the Iceman was discovered in 1991 by two hikers in the Alps, and how the remains were later taken to a laboratory for study. Then in Part Two, the author presents "The Iceman's Story: How It Might Have Been," drawing on the evidence unearthed in the remains. Here the pieced-together story is complemented by conjecture, as when we are told, "From evidence of his skull and teeth, archeologists estimate that the Iceman was between 25 and 40 years old" (p. 16).

Writers can also use information about the past and present to predict the future. Once again, the reader must be clearly informed. An example of such forecasting can be found in Sarah Gearhart's *The Telephone* (1999). After several chapters detailing the history of the telephone and its impact, a foldout insert includes predictions about what telephones might be like in the future: a phone that can "send and receive sounds, pictures, and data (e-mail) and automatically dials whomever the caller names" (unpaged foldout insert). In books that clearly distinguish the actual from the plausible, authors let their readers know that they are switching focus from the past or present to the future, thus providing a model for thinking that is clearly rooted in what is actually known.

4. Use a Nonstory Format. Another way to avoid the problem of telling a well-rounded story when the information isn't complete is not to tell a story at all. There are a number of creative nonfiction formats to choose from. For example, in the 1999 Orbis Pictus honor book *Hottest, Coldest, Highest, Deepest* (1998), author Steve Jenkins touches on the extremes—the superlatives of geography. This book dashes from one place to the next, showing readers the *longest* river, the *oldest* and *deepest* lake, the *highest* mountain and so forth. This approach leaves the reader appreciating the grandeur of the natural world.

Gold Fever! Tales from the California Gold Rush (1999) by Rosalyn Schanzer gives readers a sense of the excitement of the find, the perils of travel to California by sea or land in an earlier time, the prospecting experience, and more—all through the use of excerpts from actual letters, journals, and newspapers. Although there is a sequence of events here, and the book is divided in sections such as "An Astounding Discovery," "Ho! for California," and "Off to the Diggings," there is no single story, but rather a collage of experiences.

Using a nonstory format allows writers to present information in new and different ways not constrained by plot. Other examples of formats—alphabet format, annotated catalog, comparison and contrast—abound in current nonfiction and have been described in detail by Bamford and Kristo (1998).

Where We're Heading

Like all literature, nonfiction for children is changing in response to the times. It is incorporating many visual aspects from technology. It is delving into topics previously left untouched or topics altogether new. It is reasonable, then, to expect the telling of information to change as well, and it is changing. One of these changes involves intermingling fictional material with nonfiction literature.

Since the value and impact of fictionalized material remains controversial at present, it is likely to receive continuing attention. But as we evaluate this material, we do well to ask ourselves:

- What is the writer's responsibility to his or her material?
- Is it acceptable to seize the label of nonfiction while rejecting its truth-telling mandate?
- Do we need to broaden our notion of genre to include a new category of what has been variously called *faction*, *fictional nonfiction*, or *fuzzy texts*?

For members of the Orbis Pictus Award Committee, the truth-telling mandate of nonfiction is a nonnegotiable quality.

References

Alexander, P. (1997). Knowledge-seeking and self-schema: A case for the motivational dimensions of exposition. *Educational Psychologist, 32,* 83–94.

Bamford, R. A., & Kristo, J. V. (1998). Choosing quality nonfiction literature: Examining aspects of accuracy and organization. In R. A. Bamford & J. V. Kristo (Eds.), *Making facts come alive: Choosing quality nonfiction literature K–8* (pp. l9–38). Norwood, MA: Christopher-Gordon.

Carvajal, D. (1998, February 24). Now! Read the true (more or less) story! *The New York Times,* pp. E1, E4.

Caswell, L. J., & Duke, N. K. (1998). Non-narrative as a catalyst for literacy development. *Language Arts, 75,* 108–17.

Colman, P. (1999). Nonfiction is literature, too. *The New Advocate, 12,* 215–23.

Cummins, J. (1998). Storyographies: A new genre? *School Library Journal, 44*(8), 42–43.

Freedman, R. (1998). On telling the truth. *Booklist, 95,* 224–25.

Jenkins, C. B. (1999). *The allure of authors: Author studies in the elementary classroom.* Portsmouth, NH: Heinemann.

Leal, D. J. (1995). When it comes to informational storybooks, the end of the story has not yet been written: Response to Zarnowski's article. *The New Advocate, 8,* 197–201.

Martinez, M., & Nash, M. (1998). Children's books: A look at how we evaluate and select them. *Journal of Children's Literature, 24,* 6–19.

Oates, J. C. (1998, February 26). Believing what we read, and vice versa. *The New York Times,* p. A23.

Pappas, C. C., Kiefer, B. Z., & Levstik, L. (1999). *An integrated language perspective in the elementary school: An action approach* (3rd ed.). New York: Longman.

Sterngold, J. (1998, December 26). Just like real life? Well, maybe a little more exciting. *The New York Times,* pp. B7, B9.

Yagoda, B. (1998, March 15). In cold facts, some books falter. *The New York Times,* sec. 4, p. 6.

Children's Books

Aliki. (1999). *William Shakespeare & the Globe.* New York: HarperCollins.

Armstrong, J. (1998). *Shipwreck at the bottom of the world: The extraordinary true story of Shackleton and the* Endurance. New York: Crown.

Blumberg, R. (1998). *What's the deal? Jefferson, Napoleon, and the Louisiana Purchase.* Washington, DC: National Geographic Society.

Gearhart, S. (1999). *The telephone.* Foldout illus. T. Welles. New York: Atheneum.

Gillette, J. L. (1997). *Dinosaur ghosts: The mystery of Coelophysis.* Ill. D. Henderson. New York: Dial Books.

Hampton, W. (1997). *Kennedy assassinated! The world mourns: A reporter's story.* Cambridge, MA: Candlewick Press.

Harness, C. (1998). *Ghosts of the White House.* New York: Simon & Schuster.

Jenkins, S. (1998). *Hottest, coldest, highest, deepest.* Boston: Houghton Mifflin.

Montgomery, S. (1999). *The snake scientist.* Illus. N. Bishop. Boston: Houghton Mifflin.

Peacock, L. (1998). *Crossing the Delaware: A history in many voices.* New York: Atheneum.

Pringle, L. (1997). *An extraordinary life: The story of a monarch butterfly.* Illus. B. Marstall. New York: Orchard Books.

Ringgold, F. (1999). *If a bus could talk: The story of Rosa Parks.* New York: Simon & Schuster.

Schanzer, R. (1999). *Gold fever! Tales from the California Gold Rush.* Washington, DC: National Geographic Society.

Stanley, D., & Vennema, P. (1992). *Bard of Avon: The story of William Shakespeare.* Illus. D. Stanley. New York: Morrow.

Tanaka, S. (1996). *Discovering the Iceman: What was it like to find a 5,300-year-old mummy?* Illus. L. McGaw. New York: Hyperion.

Yolen, J., & Stemple, H. (1999). *The Mary Celeste: An unsolved mystery from history.* Illus. R. Roth. New York: Simon & Schuster.

Nonfiction Book Design in a Digital Age

Richard M. Kerper
Millersville University

From Comenius's *Orbis Sensualium Pictus*[1] to the nonfiction published in the twenty-first century, handheld books have offered readers opportunities to learn about their world as well as the larger universe of which it is a small part. The printed word has connected us to ideas, places, and events from the past and to those in contemporary life. The visual display—a double spread, inset, diagram, or map—has allowed us to see what our lives do not connect us to directly and to understand relationships between these things. But today this familiar face of nonfiction is undergoing radical changes (Dresang, 1999; Dresang & McClelland, 1999).

The Changing Face of Nonfiction

For many years, most nonfiction books for older children contained a written text that was organized into neatly developed paragraphs with topic sentences and ran from front cover to back cover. If the sequence was broken, it was only for the occasional picture, map, or diagram to which the text referred. Therefore, many consumers read the book from cover to cover or, if looking for specific information, used the index to read the most relevant segments. Even books that were heavily illustrated for the young child were organized in a first-page-to-last-page manner. Thus, for many children reading was a linear process. But for some, it was a recursive process that involved dipping in and returning to relevant pieces of visual or print material, often embedded in a general movement from front to back cover (Kerper, 1995). Many of us on the Orbis Pictus Award Committee are quite comfortable with a linear approach to experiencing and using nonfiction. For years the nature of the handheld book has supported this approach. But in recent years, we have been encountering books that do not appear to be this straightforward.

This work is supported in part by a grant from Millersville University of Pennsylvania.

In *A Tree Is Growing* (Dorros, 1997), S. D. Schindler's etched and colored pencil drawings depict a developing white oak as an exemplar of the general description of tree growth found in the main text. Sidebars visually and textually provide related information about other trees and elaborate on growth processes. Through the photographs and letters laid out in *Anastasia's Album* (Brewster, 1996), we discover snippets of the life that the grand duchess of Russia led prior to the bloody Bolshevik takeover. The main text provides a brief overview, but the photos set at an angle on top of the primary photograph create a montage of this royal life.

In Peter Sis's *Starry Messenger* (1996), a simple but engaging linear text presents a limited biography of Galileo Galilei. Word pictures that shape the writing of Galileo and his contemporaries into script images of the topic at hand up the ante on what this book has to offer. Galileo's words about the creation of a telescope take on the shape of that instrument. His thoughts about scientific investigation create the shape of an eye, while his head is trapped inside as the eye's pupil. On this page, the main text notes that Galileo remained under house arrest for the remainder of his life, but neither detention nor blindness prevented him from circulating his ideas. Thus, the word picture rapidly conveys the idea that the main text introduces. After all, visuals communicate simultaneously, whereas print communicates sequentially.

A Dorling Kindersley volume, *The Snake Book* (Ling & Atkinson, 1997), whose oversized pages contribute to the breathtaking impact of the images, shows us double-spread color photographs of twelve snakes. The print winds its way through the body of each snake—rising, falling, and rising in size—simulating the serpentine movement of this reptile (see Figure 3.1). The last page displays miniature images of the different snakes found in the book and for each provides its size, food, hunting method, geographic distribution worldwide, and scientific name.

In *Information and Book Learning*, Margaret Meek (1996) cites the underlying philosophy stated in the promotional materials for the Dorling Kindersley books:

> Pictures are presented in great detail to "slow down the looking," in ways not possible on television, so that the reader investigates the details on the page, and, at the same time, to "speed up the reading" by keeping the words close to the icons and making the bursts of printed text as short as possible, so as to fix what the reader sees in his or her memory. (p. 46)

This focus on the visual presentation of material is not unique to Dorling Kindersley publications, although their presentational style, popularized in the Eyewitness series, is distinct.

Figure 3.1.
The Symbolic Nature of Print
in *The Snake Book*

The Californian king snake . . .

has a penchant for
eating other snakes—they're
the perfect shape to swallow!
It is even prepared to take
on the deadly rattlesnake.
Immune to the poison
of the rattler, the king snake has little
to fear. Californian king snakes are
polymorphic—some are black and white, others
are brown and cream; some have stripes, others have rings.

It is clear that book designers "pay as much attention, sometimes more, to what readers look at as to what they read" (Meek, 1996, p. 44). So as we encounter these and many other variations of what we have come to know as the nonfiction book, we find ourselves wondering whether these changes make a positive contribution to nonfiction books. Does unconventional use of print or a nonlinear style of presentation communicate information to children?

As the Dorling Kindersley philosophy points out, the presentation of visual and linguistic material has an impact on the consumer. Traditionally, we have thought of book consumers as *readers,* a term connoting one who is focused on words. But books for children contain much more than unadorned text, as the previous examples demonstrate. Design decisions for presenting text, as well as the varied visual means of displaying information, make viewing as important a process as reading. So I have chosen to use the term *viewer-reader* in my discussion in order to keep both processes before us as we consider nonfiction and its consumers.

Affordance in a Digital World

The opportunities, or affordances (Gibson, 1979), for viewing or reading that a nonfiction book provides are dependent on two factors—the characteristics of the printed word and visual presentation, and the characteristics and purposes of the viewer-reader (Looren de Jong, 1991). As previously stated, for centuries the print and visual displays in handheld books were linear and sequential in design. The printed text followed a single path of thought, and the visuals—pictures, maps, and tables—extended or clarified the information. People created each book with a clear vision of its use in mind. For readers in the industrial age, this assembly line approach matched their view of the world and their way of mentally organizing it. But with the advent of television in the early part of the twentieth century and its public availability by midcentury came the beginning of fundamental changes in society. Suddenly the world was more easily connected. A global society began to emerge. This trend continued into the latter part of the century with the availability of electronic media—a digital form using bytes and bits. With this change to a digital age came a resultant nonlinear and nonsequential way of experiencing the world. Branching processes became a dominant way of thinking—a result of what computer technology offered. This highly visual medium fostered greater consumer interactivity. Learners became used to the control that pointing and clicking gave them in the electronic environment. These fundamental changes in society have helped create consumers of nonfiction who are very different from the original readers of Hendrik Van Loon's inaugural Newbery Award–winning history of the world, *The Story of Mankind* (1921).

Today's young readers are more visually oriented. They have grown up watching television as well as experiencing the virtual realities that modern technology offers. Using electronic resources, they have made decisions continuously in their search for information. Unlike linearly organized books, information in electronic formats is fluid; it is not frozen in a linear sequence. Thus, today's viewer-reader comes to the handheld book with different expectations and purposes that are framed differently than those of the first readers of Van Loon's history. Consequently, as authors, illustrators, and designers of children's nonfiction create new books, changes in our understanding of "use" and "user" must be taken into account.

Book Design in the Twentieth Century

In response to the changing nature of today's viewer-reader, book designers have created handheld books that are structured like digital texts. They have made them more interactive, enabling children to "point and click" with their eyes (Dresang, 1999). Sidebars, like those in *A Tree Is Growing* (Dorros, 1997), may be explored in conjunction with the main text, or they may be ignored totally or returned to later. Unconventional fonts, like that in *The Snake Book* (Ling & Atkinson, 1997), may be considered for their symbolic offerings, or the text may be read in a literal and linear fashion. These design features are not a phenomenon of the 1990s: "The shift to the visual as a means of communication with a validity equal to that of the verbal, date[s] back to the late 1960s or early 1970s" (Dresang, 1999, p. 29), resulting from the instant connectivity that television introduced to U.S. homes. What is new is the degree to which digital-age features are appearing in books for children. But even some of these features predate the introduction of television to the home and emerged spontaneously, becoming prototypes for today's designs.

Figure 3.2.
Page Design in *Minn of the Mississippi*

THE FEMALE ALLIGATOR, UNLIKE MOST REPTILES, GUARDS HER 3-INCH, OBLONG EGGS BURIED DEEPLY IN A MOUND OF HEAPED-UP RUSHES, LEAVES AND TWIGS.

Sam and Robert followed the riverbank, Minn swung from the pole like a frying pan and a yellow noise spinning in circles was the dog. When the boys stopped to rest, Minn struck again. This time she seemed to be growing a yellow mustache.

"That dawg goin' be full-blood hairless, mighty soon," Sam sighed. "Now, past them bushes — now over this chicken wire — there you go, Tuttle, to th' puddle."

"But she shies *away* from the puddle!" said Robert. "What's *in* that pond?"

"Look down from here," said Sam, walking around to a plank pushed over the water like a diving board. "That big lump down there is a 'loggerhaid.' Named 'cuz his haid is like th' end of a log, I reckon. But a travelin' man, he say to Pappy, '*Real* loggerhaids is sea-tuttles, like in th' Gulf. This is a *alligator* tuttle.' But Pappy say, 'We got 'gator gar-fish, they kills good fish. We got real 'gators in swamps, they eats hawgs. Ah jes' don' wanna hear no mo' bout '*gators!* In this here fambly, this here tuttle is jes' plain *loggerhaid!*'

"Pappy an' Gran'pap, they caught him in th' swamp, fetched him by wagon. He more'n two foot wide, over a hundred pound, too big fer a swill-bar'l — so we made this tuttle-pen. When we turned him loose in it, Pappy stepped on his back, an' he walked off with Pappy to th' puddle, easy! Pappy held a crotch stick to chuck his haid down, did he snap backward. That haid's eight inches wide — could snap Pappy's foot clean off, one bite! He goin' be a big kettle of stew at a County Fair come fall. An' you thought that li'l ole snapper was a *whopper,* huh? Why Robert, 'longside that big ole loggerhaid she's a itty-bitty, gentle kitten!"

That night, painful yelps called the family from the cabin to the turtle pen.

"*That dawg!*" yelled Sam, pointing to a hole under pushed-up wire. "Feudin' agin'! Dug under to git that snapper, but *she* come out! Yaller hair all aroun' ——"

"BOTH TUTTLES GOT LOOSE!" bellowed Gran'pap. "CRAWLED UNDER DE FENCE! IF'N DAT WAS *MY* DAWG ——" But that dog was now a full-blooded pointer again. Down at the riverbank, like a statue set on a plank, his nose was pointed at disappearing bubbles.

THE GAR FISH (OR GAR PIKE) IS ONE OF OUR OLDEST FISHES. IT IS A "GAN-OID" WITH BONY PLATES INSTEAD OF SCALES. IT IS TRULY AN ANCIENT, DESTRUCTIVE AND VICIOUS MONSTER FROM A SAVAGE PAST. ALLIGATOR GARS GROW TO TEN FEET.

ANYONE REALLY INTERESTED IN TURTLES SHOULD READ "TURTLES OF THE UNITED STATES AND CANADA" BY CLIFFORD H. POPE.

70

MINN

THE ALLIGATOR SNAPPER, CALLED "LOGGERHEAD"

THE REAL LOGGERHEAD OF THE SEA

Take a look at a page from a book written by Holling Clancy Holling in the 1940s and 1950s, reproduced in Figure 3.2.

In *Minn of the Mississippi* (Holling, 1951), a Newbery honor book, every margin is filled. We find

- pictures of turtles and other fauna and flora of the region
- maps of the river and lakes

- tables of the region's history
- cross section diagrams of a turtle's nest and of the locks and dams
- a pie diagram of the turtle's food sources
- a flow diagram of a turtle's embryonic development

While the main text can be read in a linear way, the decision to view-read the material in the margins can enrich the experience and the information the book provides. The marginal material offers multiple paths through the book. Thus, this design feature afforded midcentury viewer-readers the opportunity to construct their own text based on what they chose to attend to and what they chose to ignore, just as it affords today's viewer-reader the same opportunity.

The reuse of groundbreaking designs connects the work of artists and designers steeped in the history of children's book design to the best of early children's book design. In the 1998 Orbis Pictus Award winner, *An Extraordinary Life: The Story of a Monarch Butterfly* (Pringle, 1997), artist Bob Marstall and designer Hans Teensma drew on the work of Holling Clancy Holling and his design team to create a book for the digital-age viewer-reader. Marstall acknowledges,

> For me a major influence was Holling Clancy Holling. *Minn of the Mississippi* was the origin of the Monarch book. . . . So, the format came with a lot of side images and information. Of course, we modified and simplified it. Holling's stuff is dense; practically every margin is filled. We took a modified approach. The book was really inspired by the idea of the journey and by the design of the book. (Kerper, 1999, p. 3; see Figure 3.3)

Just as the decision about page layout creates an intertextual connection, so too does the font choice for *An Extraordinary Life*. Teensma notes that he chose a classic typeface because it captured the appearance of a Holling book. He goes on to state, "I believe books are going to be around much longer than we are. It's nice to know someone is going to come across a book one day and notice [the connection to the past]. Then, I feel I have done the right thing, taken publishing a step farther" (Kerper, 1999, pp. 13–14).

Not all recent nonfiction has such an obvious historical connection. The design for many books appears to be a product of the late twentieth century. In *Safari beneath the Sea: The Wonder World of the North Pacific Coast*, Diane Swanson (1994) includes boxed information on outside margins, bulleted high-interest facts at the end of chapters, and boldly captioned undersea color photographs throughout. Closely related to but going beyond the main text, these features afford viewer-readers opportunities to explore subtopics in more depth if their purposes align with the book's offerings. They permit, and actually invite, nonlinear, nonsequential exploration.

Figure 3.3.
Page Design in *An Extraordinary Life*

stalk called a cremaster had developed within her body when she was a caterpillar. A knob on the end of the cremaster was covered with scores of tiny hooks facing in all directions. Danaus had to twist the knob of the cremaster to snag the hooks on to the silk mat so that her chrysalis would be firmly stuck to the stem. If she failed, the legs of her old skin would soon dry up and let go of the mat. She would fall to the ground and lie there helpless, with no chance of emerging successfully as a butterfly.

Still head down and sightless, Danaus used her muscles to twist the cremaster up around her old skin. She pushed it up toward the stem. There! She felt the knob hook on to the silk! For a moment she swiveled violently, driving more of the cremaster's hooks into the mat. Then she stopped moving. The walls of her chrysalis slowly hardened around her.

Held to the stem by its strong black stalk, the chrysalis looked like a jade jewel studded with tiny gold gems. It hung motionless and well camouflaged among the stems and leaves of the hayfield.

A monarch butterfly develops within its chrysalis over a span of five to fifteen days, depending on the temperature. Danaus's mother had been a midsummer pupa; for her the pupation process had lasted just nine days. But now summer was nearly over. The days grew shorter. Some nights were cool enough to chill the crickets and katydids, slowing their calls. The cool temperatures slowed the pace of change within Danaus's chrysalis.

Nevertheless, within twelve days she had changed dramatically: from a creature that walked on sixteen legs and ate leaves to one that would fly on four wings and sip liquids from flowers. Her trusty cutting mouthparts were replaced by a hollow drinking tube. Her caterpillar digestive system that had broken down thousands of milkweed bites was no longer needed. It was replaced by a much smaller and

17

The old skin first splits open at the bottom (head) end. As the split widens, a butterfly pupa wriggles free of its old caterpillar skin.

The cremaster stalk of the pupa holds it firmly to the silk mat spun by the caterpillar.

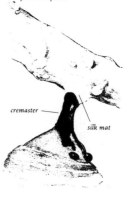

cremaster —

silk mat

Similarly, Patricia Lauber's *Hurricanes: Earth's Mightiest Storms* (1996) includes occasional blue pages that stand out from the white pages of the main text. These blue pages provide visual and textual displays that make possible further investigation of subtopics such as weather instruments, hurricane naming, and famous hurricanes, which the main text mentions but does not develop. In *The Bone Detectives: How Forensic Anthropologists Solve Crimes and Uncover*

Mysteries of the Dead, Donna Jackson (1996) inserts pages titled "Forensic File." Each one visually and textually provides information that viewer-readers might want to know as they attempt to understand how forensic anthropologists solve a real murder mystery by identifying a victim through reconstruction from human remains. And, in *The Top of the World: Climbing Mount Everest*, Steve Jenkins (1999) includes collage-formed boxes along the sides and bottoms and in the corners of pages. These set-off features provide visual and print information about the formation, measurement, and naming of the mountain, the attempts to climb to the peak, and the dangers faced by climbers, while the main text chronicles the major factors affecting an attempt to climb to the top. In each case, viewer-readers are empowered to determine the order in which they encounter ideas and to reformulate that order based on changing purposes.

Whereas these books are highly successful in speaking to digital-age viewer-readers, others speak to an audience with a different orientation. In *Mapping the World* (1999), Sylvia A. Johnson surveys the history of mapmaking. Each section presents a step in the chronology. Images of ancient and modern maps in each part of the history are clearly referenced in the text. Thus, the book's linear, sequential structure invites the same type of reading and viewing. Viewer-readers' opportunities to determine how they encounter the material are much more limited.

By contrast, the picture book *Gorilla Walk* (1999) by Ted Lewin and Betsy Lewin chronicles the fulfillment of the dreams of this husband and wife team—meeting the mountain gorilla in the Impenetrable Forest of Uganda. In addition to single- and double-page watercolors, the book's pages are sprinkled with illustrations in the margins, some with captions, others without. While some pictures illustrate or extend what the text details, others have no clear link to the words on the page. On pages 6 and 7, for example, the print focuses on the habituation of mountain gorillas (i.e., making them comfortable in the presence of humans) and the problems involved in ecotourism. The text makes no reference to any other animals, yet the drawings depict fifteen other forms of wildlife. Thus, for many viewer-readers a potential affordance is not realized because the main text does not provide a link to the marginalia. The drawings serve primarily a decorative function, even though most are clearly labeled, because their relationship to the mountain gorilla is not established.

Clearly, then, some book designs work well, while others are less successful. What the best creations share is a clear link between the visual/design elements and the linguistic ones. They establish what Stuart Murphy refers to as a partnership in which the visuals work "'with the words to create a text'" (cited in LaSpina, 1998, p. 31). These are what Steve Moline (1995) calls *integrated texts*—texts in which "parts support, explain or give context to one another" (p. 14).

Conclusion

Today's young viewer-readers are a product of a new age. Technological advances of the late twentieth century help to shape their thought processes differently than did the influences that shaped ours. So book designs that seem disorganized to us may only be organized differently. What may seem unclear or "busy" to us may be crystal clear when seen through another, generally younger, lens. Therefore, when we look at new ways of presenting information in nonfiction books, we need to resist a knee-jerk reaction. We must consider the culture that has shaped our children and must try to view these books as children will experience them. Our students are the intended audience. As teachers we must seriously consider the purposes and characteristics of the viewer-reader when developing curriculum. If this requires expansion of our ways of seeing and thinking, then let's get on with it. Let's help our children develop the flexibility to experience and understand the diversity that exists in handheld books.

Note

1. In 1657 Johannes Amos Comenius published in Latin and High Dutch what is reputed to be the first illustrated, informational text for children. The book is titled *Orbis sensualium pictus: Hoc est omnium principalium in mundo rerum, et in vita actionum, pictura & nomenclatura.* The translation of the Latin is *The Visible World: or A Nomenclature, and Pictures of All the Chief Things That Are in the World, and of Men's Employments Therein,* according to G. E. Littlefield in *Early Schools and School-Books of New England* (New York: Russell & Russell, 1904/1965). The main title has been shortened to *Orbis Pictus* in many recent texts and in NCTE's award for children's nonfiction.

References

Dresang, E. T. (1999). *Radical change: Books for youth in a digital age.* New York: H. W. Wilson.

Dresang, E. T., & McClelland, K. (1999). Radical change: Digital age literature and learning. *Theory into Practice, 38*(3), 160–67.

Gibson, J. J. (1979). *The ecological approach to visual perception.* Boston: Houghton Mifflin.

Kerper, R. M. (1995). Three children viewing and reading: Transactions with illustrations and print in informational books. (Doctoral dissertation, The Ohio State University, 1994). *Dissertation Abstracts International, 56* (01-A) [Online]. (University Microfilms No. AADAA-I9517029)

Kerper, R. M. (1999). *Collaborating on nonfiction: Author, illustrator and designer.* Manuscript in preparation.

LaSpina, J. A. (1998). *The visual turn and the transformation of the textbook.* Mahwah, NJ: Lawrence Erlbaum.

Looren de Jong, H. (1991). Intentionality and the ecological approach. *Journal for the Theory of Social Behaviour, 21*(1), 91–109.

Meek, M. (1996). *Information and book learning.* Woodchester, England: Thimble Press.

Moline, S. (1995). *I see what you mean: Children at work with visual information.* York, ME: Stenhouse.

Children's Books

Brewster, H. (1996). *Anastasia's album.* Photo. Peter Christopher. New York: Hyperion.

Dorros, A. (1997). *A tree is growing.* Illus. S. D. Schindler. New York: Scholastic Press.

Holling, H. C. (1951). *Minn of the Mississippi.* Boston: Houghton Mifflin.

Jackson, D. M. (1996). *The bone detectives: How forensic anthropologists solve crimes and uncover mysteries of the dead.* Photo. Charlie Fellenbaum. Boston: Little, Brown.

Jenkins, S. (1999). *The top of the world: Climbing Mt. Everest.* Boston: Houghton Mifflin.

Johnson, S. A. (1999). *Mapping the world.* New York: Atheneum.

Lauber, P. (1996). *Hurricanes: Earth's mightiest storms.* New York: Scholastic Press.

Lewin, T., & Lewin, B. (1999). *Gorilla walk.* New York: Lothrop, Lee and Shepard.

Ling, M., & Atkinson, M. (1997). *The snake book.* Photo. Frank Greenaway & Dave King. New York: DK Publishing.

Pringle, L. (1997). *An extraordinary life: The story of a monarch butterfly.* Illus. Bob Marstall. New York: Orchard Books.

Sis, P. (1996). *Starry messenger: A book depicting the life of a famous scientist, mathematician, astronomer, philosopher, physicist, Galileo Galilei.* New York: Farrar, Straus and Giroux.

Swanson, D. (1994). *Safari beneath the sea: The wonder world of the North Pacific Coast.* Photo. Royal British Columbia Museum. San Francisco: Sierra Club Books.

Van Loon, Hendrik. (1921). *The Story of Mankind.* Garden City, NY: Boni & Liveright.

Acknowledging, Citing, Going Beyond: Issues of Documentation in Nonfiction Literature

Karen Patricia Smith
Queens College, City University of New York

The demands of the technology age during the last decade of the twentieth century were reflected in the expectations held by the reader seeking information. The art of providing fine writing informed by factual detail does, however, place an unusual responsibility on the author. During the first decade of the award's existence, Orbis Pictus Award–winning books increasingly showed evidence of author regard for scholarship and documentation.

Author Responsibility

The nonfiction writer of distinction actively engages the attention of the youthful audience, attempting to balance fact and stimulating narrative with attractive format and illustrations. But this balance would be nonexistent were it not for the author's attention to process. Part of that process involves sharing with the audience the origins of the information. As Myra Zarnowski has indicated in her essay in this volume (Chapter 2), in nonfiction works there must be a clear differentiation between fact and fiction; while they may be interesting to read, "factions" are at best deceptive, and they are unacceptable to those seeking accurate interpretations of events, issues, and phenomena. Evidence of careful documentation supports the well-conceived nonfiction presentation.

Currently, we are witnessing a national emphasis on raising educational standards with an eye toward setting the baseline for accountability for both education professionals and students. Nonfiction authors are confronted by inquisitive and demanding readers who not only examine texts for information about a chosen topic, but also expect to see evidence of the source material from which the information has been taken. In an age in which ethics seem in short supply, authors have a strong responsibility to act as role models for the young. Margery Fisher, author of the first full-length study of nonfiction, stated as early as 1972 that "formally or informally, an information book sets out to teach. . . . Trends in nonfiction have followed trends in education, not always with advantage" (p. 15). Nonfiction authors must be cognizant, then, of the unique role they can play in the nonfiction craft by helping to develop the information base of young people.

Given the sophisticated needs of contemporary youth, the line between the scholarly expectations of the adult audience and the fulfillment of young readers' knowledge needs has become somewhat blurred. That nonfiction narrative be supported by verifiable detail is considered an expectation rather than an ornament. The larger issue is actually that of intellectual debt. Garfield (1996) has stated: "When editors and scholars are asked about citation practices, they are primarily concerned as to whether authors have acknowledged intellectual debts. Such acknowledgment is widely believed to be fundamental to ethical scholarly behavior" (p. 450). Showing evidence of intellectual debt, then, is no longer the sole domain of the author of adult nonfiction.

What Careful Citing Can Do for the Young Reader

The citing of resources is an important aspect of information gathering specifically and of credible research in general. The Orbis Pictus Award Committee carefully examines works submitted for nomination for evidence of sound scholarship. Garfield has identified conditions under which it is important to cite the sources of information. These include:

1 paying homage to pioneers
2 giving credit for related work
3 substantiating claims
4 providing background reading
5 identifying original publications in which an idea or concept was discussed (1996, pp. 451–52)

These elements are particularly relevant in nonfiction writing for young people and are referred to in the following paragraphs.

In *The Great American Gold Rush* (1989), Rhoda Blumberg supports a fascinating narrative with careful documentation. Were it not for the diaries and memoirs left us by the people who lived the experience—namely, the miners themselves—we would have little firsthand information about their emotions, motivations, and responses. While the gold rush itself is a memorable part of U.S. history, it is the connection of people to events that makes the record so powerful. Good journalism can also add much to the historical record. Blumberg shares with her audience some of the observations of Bayard Taylor, a newspaperman who covered the story for the New York *Herald*. His words and views help to substantiate the fact that the gold rush greatly affected and forever altered the lives of the people involved.

Some of those headed west took what was considered a shortcut—a ship to Panama, land transport across Panama, and another ship to California. Taylor wrote of having seen a woman from Maine fording a stream aided by two Panamanian natives, who held on to her so that the waist-high torrential waters wouldn't carry her away (Blumberg, 1989, p. 26). His observations capture the drama of the incident as well as his amazement at seeing a woman so caught up in the frenzy of gold fever that she dared to travel alone on such a potentially dangerous mission. The woman's situation is further underscored by the fact that she must ultimately rely on the assistance of strange men. In providing this reference, which is documented through an endnote, Blumberg both supports her belief that these were dangerous, exciting, and memorable times and gives credit to the experience of Bayard Taylor. Although in this case Blumberg does not quote directly from the newspaper, she supports the statement through reference to Taylor's book *Eldorado; or, Adventures in the Path of Empire* (1949). Thus, readers learn that in a case such as this, there can be more than one primary source. Blumberg's regard for scholarship is reflected in the organization of the back matter for this book. Each chapter contains individual endnote references. Some are content notes, which go beyond the simple recording of the source to offer additional or ancillary information about the subject. It is helpful to learn through one content endnote, for example, that only 2 percent of the populace present at the gold digs were women. We understand even better, then, Taylor's wonderment at the scene by the stream in Panama. In another reference, we discover that one gold rush participant, a doctor by trade, took fortuitous advantage of the freezing weather he encountered on the way to the mine fields; by adding peppermint oil to the milk from his cows, he inadvertently created ice cream! Thus, readers learn that there is more information available than is provided in the main text, and that some information may be contained within a content footnote.

It is interesting to note that in an earlier work, *Sharks* (1976), Blumberg, who so carefully documented resources in subsequent books, was actually criticized by some for what were deemed "lightweight observation[s]" (Carter & Abrahamson, 1990, p. 33) in describing the swimming habits of sharks as follows: "They don't always cruise along calmly. Sometimes they leap out of the water. One of these big, heavy giants was seen jumping so high that its tail was six feet above the water" (Blumberg, 1976, p. 37). Referring to this "observation," Carter and Abrahamson comment, "This casual allusion prompts several unanswerable questions. Who saw the shark? Was this person a reliable judge of distances, particularly over water? Could this person accurately identify a basking shark?" (p. 33). Indeed, while it may seem surprising that this observation came from the pen of a now-acclaimed author, it is refreshing for the young (and old alike) to see how Blumberg grew as a nonfiction author, fine-tuning her research techniques over the years.

Citing sources and offering additional information through footnotes, however, is only half the process. A really good nonfiction writer provides a detailed bibliography that offers the full name of author, title of work, publisher, and place and date of publication. In *The Great American Gold Rush*, Blumberg further divides her resources into primary and secondary categories. This is helpful for readers, especially when firsthand accounts are involved, because we can easily see the difference between primary and secondary resources. Blumberg's respect for the scholarly process is clearly illustrated in her documentation. Such detail was obviously not lost on the Orbis Pictus Award Committee members; *The Great American Gold Rush* was a 1990 Orbis Pictus honor book.

Some cautions are in order, however, regarding total reliance on certain firsthand accounts. Historian Bernard Bailyn, writing about documentation in *On the Teaching and Writing of History* (1994), reminds us that:

> Sources are always changing and are always suspect. Newspapers became a source of evidence in the eighteenth century, but they too have to be used critically and cautiously. Eighteenth-century newspapers were very often hackwork by hired writers. If you think of the eighteenth-century newspapers as small versions of today's *New York Times*, you're in trouble—because they weren't. Most of them, financed by partisan interests, didn't even pretend to objectivity. Their printers had their own agendas, and the modern historian must use them partly for the information they contain about the events that they describe and partly, too, as evidence of their writers' biases and agendas. (p. 46)

Therefore, it is always reassuring and crucial to see different types of resources reflected in a bibliographical listing. Author Jean Fritz, herself the winner of the Orbis Pictus Award in 1990, has stated that "there can be no understanding of history without coming to terms with the makers and shakers. . . . Enough of their personal record must be available so that I can attempt to figure out why they became who they were" (1995, p. 257). This is the kind of information that an alert teacher or school media specialist can point out to young readers, helping them to become better researchers. It is the kind of information that Orbis Pictus Award Committee members look for when considering a work of nonfiction for the award.

Documentation and the Issue of Cultural Sensitivity

No discussion of documentation could be complete without at least a brief mention of the debate regarding the relationship of documentation to cultural sensitivity. Although many have addressed aspects of this issue (Bishop, 1982; Johnson-Feelings, 1990; Smith, 1994; Vanasse, 1998), it is difficult (if not impossible) to reach consensus about whether one must be a member of the racial or ethnic group about whom one is writing, and whether one must indicate this within the narrative. In an article appearing in the November 1991 Book Review section of the *New York Times*, noted author and educator Henry Louis Gates Jr. suggested that whether an individual from a particular ethnic group has actually authored a piece is not always immediately discernible; authorship, he indicates, can be manipulated in a way that deceives the public.

Over the years, books by minority authors have been represented among the committee's final choices for recommended reading; these include books by Virginia Hamilton, Patricia C. McKissack and Fredrick McKissack, Andrea Davis Pinkney, Pat Cummings, Arthur Dorros, and Junko Morimoto, among others, though to date only two have had works chosen for honor status: *Arctic Memories* (1990) by Normee Ekoomiak and *Christmas in the Big House, Christmas in the Quarters* (1994) by Patricia C. McKissack and Fredrick McKissack.

Ekoomiak's work is notable for being one of the few publications by a native Inuit. It succeeds in documenting firsthand the experience of Inuit tradition. Illustrations by the author serve also as cultural documentation, since illustration is so much a part of this cultural tradition. Ekoomiak is one of few Inuit individuals who have written for young people and have been successful in publishing within the mainstream press.

Russell Freedman is noted for his works about Native American cultures. A prolific writer of outstanding abilities, his work has appeared seven times on Orbis Pictus lists of outstanding nonfiction choices. He won the award in 1991 for *Franklin Delano Roosevelt* (1990), and his *The Life and Death of Crazy Horse* (1996) was chosen as an honor book in 1997. The second work is of particular note because it sensitively presents the life of this controversial Native American, partially through the use of "picture histories." As Freedman states, these were drawings accompanied by text, usually "drawn on deerskin, buffalo, or elk hide, or later, on cloth or paper, in the pages of ledger books, [telling] the stories of battles, hunts, ceremonies . . . and all sorts of memorable happenings" (1996, p. 152). Freedman uses no footnotes within his text, but he refers to specific details, incidents, and dates of events. At the conclusion of the book, he provides a discussion about the picture histories, stating that these were done by a member of the Oglala Sioux tribe. The chronology provided at the conclusion of the work is especially helpful given developmental considerations in comprehending the concept of time. The more involved the life of a key figure, the more difficult the task of sorting out the order in which events occurred and deeds took place. Freedman's chronology provides historical verification and allows the young reader to place events in perspective. The fact that Freedman utilized picture histories rather than contemporary artist renderings is particularly impressive and did not go unnoticed by the committee in its decision-making process. Despite the fact that Freedman is not Native American, he has made a clear effort to get as close to his subject as possible through sensitive scholarship.

Whetting the Appetite

The issue of documentation goes deeper than citing and labeling. It is also a means through which the author has an opportunity to whet the reader's appetite. Margaret Meek Spencer (1996) discusses the importance of providing stimulus for readers to go beyond their immediate needs for information:

> When we read in order to understand something more, or more clearly, about the world, the result is not a straightforward addition to the store of information we believe we already possess. Instead it is an increase in our confidence that we have sorted something out: a belief that we can cope with another thing we have to do, or that we possess a better understanding of the world as a whole and our life in it. We began this sorting out when we were quite young. We see children doing it all the time, especially when they begin to read. Their world is different. We can't do their thinking for them. But we can take a look at their coming to know, their learning from the books we give them and the texts they choose for themselves, to see if these are really as helpful as they might be. (p. 13)

A good nonfiction work can assist this need to "understand something more" through an excellent bibliography that does more than merely list resources mentioned in the work (a baseline of expectation). A thoughtfully constructed recommended reading list can take readers that step further.

Jim Murphy's *The Great Fire* (1995), winner of the 1996 Orbis Pictus Award, offers such an opportunity. After a stimulating account of how the 1871 Chicago fire began and its impact on those whose lives it touched, Murphy presents readers with a bibliography that is divided into two parts: first, "Sources of Accounts Presented in This Book," and then, "Other Books about the Chicago Fire," in which seventeen works are listed. This conveys to the reader that there is more to learn about the subject than the information presented by Murphy. My grandmother used to say that there is "a cloth for every wearer." And for every subject out there is a child who wants to go further, a young person so intrigued with a subject or a series of events that he or she just must know more. Without such a listing, the reader is limited to what Murphy has specifically referred to in the preparation of his own account. Is not "going beyond" one of the basic desired outcomes of education? Providing such a model can encourage young learners to go further, perhaps initiating an interest that in some way will affect what he or she chooses to investigate in the future.

Patricia Lauber's *Seeing Earth from Space* (1990), a 1991 Orbis Pictus honor book, also encourages further investigation of subject matter. Lauber provides the reader with a glossary of terms that, readers are told, refers specifically to the way terms are used in this book (p. 76). This allows the reader to more thoroughly grasp the subject at hand, which encourages greater understanding of the subject matter, as well as motivating the reader to want to know more. Lauber follows the glossary with a brief Further Reading section in which she indicates by asterisk books written with young readers in mind; others are presented for either the interest of the educator or as information sources for the more sophisticated younger reader.

"Interest" is a state of mind that develops over time; it may be a relatively short time, or an undefined, gradually developing period during which something arrests the attention of the reader about a subject, something that goes beyond a mere catching of the eye. Margaret Meek Spencer distinguishes between "*being* interested" and "*becoming* interested" (1996, p. 10). In the first case, adults assume that an interest has developed when the child's eye lingers on the text or illustrations of a book. Spencer goes on to differentiate "becoming" from "being" interested:

> Becoming interested in a more prolonged sense is a gradual realization that some discovery learning is worth pursuing beyond its immediate modishness. It commands a different kind of adherence which helps the learner . . . especially when the mastery of craft or knowledge is an object of desire. (p. 11)

Orbis Pictus selections stimulate the interests and meet the needs of the reader-audience.

The Subject "Speaks"

How do we present to the young reader authentic documentation of what the subject thought and perhaps said? In cases where the subject is an object or a place, how does the author infiltrate the barrier of unfamiliarity to offer the reader the factual information that makes that subject special and intriguing? In her 1990 Orbis Pictus Award–winning *The Great Little Madison* (1989), Jean Fritz, completely at ease with her subject, uses Madison's own letters as well as correspondence sent him by contemporaries to bring the audience closer to her view of Madison the man. Men and women in power are highly complex personalities. It takes a skillful author to give spirit to thought frozen in time and to make sense of a myriad of documentary details. In Chapter 5, Fritz quotes from a letter written by Madison to his father following a congressional meeting in 1789, in which the statesman comments on the newly formed Congress and its charge: "We are in a wilderness without a single footstep to guide us. . . . Those who may follow will have an easier task" (p. 56). Here, an excerpt from a letter gives form and substance to Madison's emotions during this difficult time. As a result of quotations from Madison's own letters, the reader gains unique personal insights, which could only be surpassed if Madison could be brought back to life to speak to us directly. Letters, diaries, and memoirs thus act as other forms of primary source documentation and lend support to the author's presentation.

Likewise, the exceptional author can cause phenomena to come to life and have "the ring of truth." In her 1995 Orbis Pictus Award winner *Safari beneath the Sea: The Wonder World of the North Pacific Coast* (1994), author Diane Swanson breathes vibrancy into the mysterious underwater world of the North Pacific while offering the reader a wealth of factual information. Here, documentation takes another form. In addition to detail, supplemented by brilliant photographs by the Royal British Columbia Museum, Swanson supports fact through the use of sidebars, snippets of information singled out for special recognition within the text. Sidebars traditionally appear at the sides of the main text and are generally the places where authors supplement the text by providing information that might be too dense or too detailed to include in the main narrative. This strategy may help support the author's argument, but it may also single out particular thoughts, phrases, or terms that the author considers worthy of special attention. Swanson, for example, mentions in the main text "nudibranchs" that inhabit the sea. A sidebar (accompanied by a full-page photograph) informs the reader that "the shaggy mouse nudibranch is an ocean slug that often makes its home in beds of eelgrass" (p. 24), thus offering further evidence that there is more than one type of nudibranch. It should also be noted that the sidebar is in boldface type, further calling attention to this part of the text.

Conclusion

Providing careful documentation—use of sidebars, correspondence, a glossary, and a selective bibliography—can encourage reader interest and foster readers' information-seeking behavior. Marian Koren states in *Tell me! The Right of the Child to Information*, "[Children] are not only receivers but also seekers of information" (1999, p. 85). As such, we owe it to them to provide them with texts that at once satisfy and stimulate their inquiring minds. Orbis Pictus titles achieve this goal, fascinating the reader by bringing to life not only the subject but also the times. By serving the young reader an exceptional entrée, well-written nonfiction helps create an appetite for reading and inquiry that will last well beyond the immediate moment of gratification.

References

Bailyn, B. (1994). *On the teaching and writing of history: Responses to a series of questions.* Hanover, NH: Montgomery Endowment, Dartmouth College.

Bishop, S. R. (1982). *Shadow and substance: Afro-American experience in contemporary children's fiction.* Urbana, IL: National Council of Teachers of English.

Carter, B., & Abrahamson, R. F. (1990). *Nonfiction for young adults: From delight to wisdom.* Phoenix, AZ: Oryx Press.

Fisher, M. (1972). *Matters of fact: Aspects of non-fiction for children.* Leicester, England: Brockhampton Press.

Fritz, J. (1995). Voices of the creators: Jean Fritz. In A. Silvey (Ed)., *Children's books and their creators: An invitation to the feast of twentieth-century literature* (p. 257). Boston: Houghton Mifflin.

Garfield, E. (1996). When to cite. *Library Quarterly, 66*(4), 449–58.

Gates, H. L. Jr. (1991, November 24). "Authenticity," or the lesson of Little Tree. *New York Times Book Review*, pp. 1, 30.

Johnson-Feelings, D. (1990). *Telling tales: The pedagogy and promise of African American literature for youth.* Westport, CT: Greenwood Press.

Koren, M. (1999). *Tell me! The right of the child to information.* Den Haag, Amsterdam: NBLC Uitgeverij.

Smith, K. P. (1994). *African-American voices in young adult literature: Tradition, transition, transformation.* Metuchen, NJ: Scarecrow Press.

Spencer, M. M. (1996). *Information and book learning.* Stroud, Gloucester, England: Thimble Press.

Vanasse, D. (1998). Cultural sensitivity. In J. E Brown & E. C. Stephens (Eds), *United in diversity: Using multicultural young adult literature in the classroom* (pp. 20–22). Urbana, IL, National Council of Teachers of English.

Children's Books

Blumberg, R. (1976). *Sharks.* New York: Franklin Watts.

Blumberg, R. (1989). *The great American Gold Rush.* New York: Scholastic.

Ekoomiak, N. (1990). *Arctic memories.* New York: Henry Holt.

Freedman, R. (1990). *Franklin Delano Roosevelt.* New York: Clarion Books.

Freedman, R. (1996). *The life and death of Crazy Horse.* New York: Holiday House.

Fritz, J. (1989). *The great little Madison.* New York: G. P. Putnam's Sons.

Lauber, P. (1990). *Seeing earth from space.* New York: Orchard Books.

McKissack, P. C., & McKissack, F. (1994). *Christmas in the big house, Christmas in the quarters.* New York: Scholastic.

Murphy, J. (1995). *The great fire.* New York: Scholastic.

Swanson, D. (1994). *Safari beneath the sea: The wonder world of the North Pacific coast.* San Francisco: Sierra Club Books for Children.

5 The Significance of Topics of Orbis Pictus Award-Winning Books

Elaine M. Aoki
Bush School, Seattle, Washington

The designation of an award is evidence of something unique. Orbis Pictus Award–winning texts and honor books are distinguished from other nonfiction works by their presentation and treatment of topics and issues. Examining an award-winning text with a critical eye allows us to view the many facets of the work. Each facet, however, forms but a small part of the total image. We see the "individualness" of detail, but only when we combine all the parts and envision the entire work are we able to form a final critical assessment of the value of the contribution. Key among Orbis Pictus Award Committee concerns when assessing books are the following: What is the potential impact of this text? Is the presentation "timeless," enabling the reader to draw analogies to other events occurring in different contexts? What is the relationship of the subject to contemporary concerns? And, finally, to what extent does the text enlighten, enhance, or illuminate curricular issues? Consideration of such elements allows committee members to identify a text as one exhibiting that special potential to stimulate the interest, curiosity, and imagination of the young reader.

Defining Significance

What makes a topic significant? Are significant topics found only within designated "factual" genres such as biography, history, and science? Readers evaluate the significance of a text in light of their experiences. What makes a work significant is the degree to which the subject is part of a collective social consciousness and whether the text is accessible at precisely the right time in the life of a reader or, as in the case of the committee, a community of readers. A literary work becomes significant because the reader is able to make a timely connection to the text, fulfilling a need, which in turn leads to satisfaction. A feeling of excitement accompanies the discovery of a "significant" contribution. The reader may be led to wonder (almost enviously, perhaps!) how the author managed to create such an exemplary work.

Significance is a dynamic variable in the committee's decision-making process. It can change with time and shifting social priorities. An example of such a shift in social priorities is our thinking about the reality of African slavery and its complex, far-reaching legacy. Not surprisingly, during the nineteenth century and in fact up through the period of the civil rights movement, few honest accounts of the evil effects of slavery were available to the public and particularly to young people. In the nineteenth century, the economy of our nation benefited from the slave practice. In succeeding years, though the institution of slavery was outlawed, the American people were still not willing to openly acknowledge the cruel effects of the practice. The advent of the civil rights movement, however, changed the tide of public opinion about acknowledging the details of the slave experience and its aftereffects. The issue was now openly acknowledged and discussed in school textbooks. And as we advanced into the final quarter of the twentieth century, public acknowledgment permeated the trade books written for young people. As of this writing, there is a bill before the United States Congress advocating that a public apology for having supported, developed, and benefited from slavery be given to African American people. Now that the causes and effects of slavery have become part of our historical consciousness, well-researched nonfiction books for children that offer fresh viewpoints on the origins and effects of the "peculiar institution" would certainly be deemed "significant" contributions. Two such books are James Haskins and Kathleen Benson's *Bound for America: The Forced Migration of Africans to the New World* (1999), an Orbis Pictus recommended book for 2000, and Walter Dean Myers's *At Her Majesty's Request* (1999), an Orbis Pictus honor book for 2000.

Whether or not a subject rises to a level of importance in the eyes of readers is an even more complex issue than it first appears. It involves consideration of the broad subject categories that make up nonfiction literature, exemplified by the arts, social science, or history. Readers must consider whether a variety of these areas, crucial for young readers' general learning and knowledge, is represented in the books singled out for distinction.

In examining the broad categories of past Orbis Pictus Award winners, we note that generally they represent at least one of four categories: science and mathematics, geography, history, and the arts. A brief analysis of the honor books for the ten-year period indicates that they are equally distributed within the three areas of science, history, and biography. One conclusion we can draw is that we need more outstanding books in a wider range of nonfiction literature. Of course, next year or the year after, the committee might be presented with one or more extraordinary works that fall into categories not yet represented in the list of Orbis Pictus Award winners.

Impact: Considering the Power and/or Attractiveness of the Subject

As committee members evaluate the multiple perspectives of the texts before them, it is necessary for us to be constantly aware of the larger framework of children's nonfiction writing. Original insight is certainly a factor for consideration. Inherent in the American ideal of freedom of expression is the right to approach an issue in more than one way.

When one designates a work as significant because of its contribution to the nonfiction field, to a certain degree that choice is always relative or subjective. We need only consider the case of M. D. Lankford's *Jacks around the World* (1996), a simple book on the child's game of jacks. In 1997, when this book came to the attention of the Orbis Pictus Award Committee, we were impressed with this small 7" x 7" text with its brightly illustrated double-spread pages focusing on the development of the game and how it is played around the world. The age range of the material was certainly within the framework for committee consideration and, in fact, it met most of the other criteria. But this book, which can be placed in the "game" category, ultimately was not selected for any award. While we felt that it made a substantial contribution to nonfiction in its provision of multicultural/international insights into the historical aspects of the universal game of jacks, Lankford's book still had to compete with other nonfiction titles published the same year. These included books by notable authors such as Rhoda Blumberg (*Full Steam Ahead: The Race to Build the Transcontinental Railroad*, 1996), Russell Freedman (*The Life and Death of Crazy Horse*, 1996), and Diane Stanley (*Leonardo da Vinci*, 1996). These authors utilized themes and focused on significant social contributions through unusual and creative accounts of (1) the transcontinental railroad (complete with photography by the National Geographic Society), (2) the American Indian warrior Crazy Horse, and (3) the brilliant Leonardo da Vinci. These subjects have over time been sanctioned and validated by historians, scientists, and educators as valuable, which adds substantially to their "significance" factor. The combination of a gifted author writing on a powerful or arresting subject is a potent combination. Unless educators eventually take a different look at games in the context of curriculum and world studies, the topic of jacks remains, in relative terms, less significant.

The Timelessness of Presentation

The work of William Shakespeare has been revered since his own day not only because of the author's gifted and poetic writing, but also because of his ability to select themes, issues, and ideas that have remained "timeless" in terms of human concerns. This timelessness allows Shakespeare's plays to be performed in modern-day apparel in an urban setting as well as in sixteenth-century dress and settings. The innate versatility of his work allows it to remain relevant even though the world has changed dramatically over the past four centuries. Therefore, it is not surprising that among the outstanding titles selected by the committee for the year 1999 was the talented Aliki's informational picture book *William Shakespeare & the Globe* (1999). The timeless topic and the attractive and informative presentation was a wonderful combination. Likewise, the theme of survival and endurance against unbeatable odds is also a timeless as well as a powerful concern. Thanks to the gifted writing and meticulous research of Jennifer Armstrong, *Shipwreck at the Bottom of the World: The Extraordinary True Story of Shackleton and the* Endurance (1998) was selected as an Orbis Pictus Award winner.

Just as the experiences faced by human beings can have a timeless quality, giving them a universal significance, human beings throughout history have had similar reactions to reoccurring phenomena. Such is the case with our response to fire. Jim Murphy's *The Great Fire* (1995) immediately engages the reader's attention by focusing on an event that few would find lacking in drama or interest. In fact, the Great Fire of Chicago has stimulated so much interest over time that numerous myths have been generated about how this fire actually began. The most memorable by far is the one that attributes the origin of the fire to a lamp kicked over by Mrs. O'Leary's cow. Yet another story implied that Mrs. O'Leary set fire to her barn in revenge for having been removed from the city's relief rolls. In truth, there is no evidence to support either premise. In his book, Murphy removes the Chicago Fire from surrounding myth and places it within a factual setting, presenting information from multiple points of view. Murphy's account offers survivors' first-hand descriptions that appeared in newspaper stories. The reader becomes an invisible witness, walking the city streets, viewing the disaster from different perspectives, and ultimately learning of errors in judgment and rushes to judgment. Although the Chicago Fire took place on October 8, 1871, the subject retains a sense of drama. Jim Murphy's unique approach allows this event to transcend its nineteenth-century setting and stir the imaginations of twenty-first-century readers.

Connections to Contemporary Concerns

Related to the notion of appealing to human interest over time is the concept of relevance—that is, how is a book related to contemporary concerns? History provides us with a record of events that illustrate a progression (or regression, as the case may be) of incidents that often explain a present-day phenomenon or show us how something familiar to us originated. The building of the transcontinental railroad, for example, is a precursor to today's rapid transport capabilities.

We are also at a point historically when it is important to highlight contributions made by various ethnic groups to the building of this nation. Jim Murphy's *Across America on an Emigrant Train* (1993) is not simply the retelling of Robert Louis Stevenson's 1879 journey across the Atlantic Ocean and the United States. It is also a narration of historically significant events such as the building of the transcontinental railroad, the impact of steam travel, the contributions of Chinese Americans to the building of the railroad, the histories of ethnic communities such as the Mennonites, African Americans, Native Americans, and others. Murphy's well-written narrative of Stevenson's journey culminates in a significant contribution to children's nonfiction and won the Orbis Pictus Award for 1994.

Exposure to quality books containing multiple perspectives helps young readers develop an understanding of the cultures, practices, and values of society. Taken further, such works often illustrate the skills needed to play a productive role in modern society. Jerry Stanley's *Children of the Dust Bowl: The True Story of the School at Weedpatch Camp* (1992), which won the Orbis Pictus Award in 1993, examines the contributions of Leo Hart to the education of homeless children. Stanley's depiction of perseverance and the importance of education as a way of escaping poverty offers an important model for young people as they seek to negotiate a world dominated by fast food and the demand for quick results.

The best nonfiction transcends the author's message and encourages the audience to branch out by reading more about the topic. We need to teach our young readers what is worth knowing; who is a reliable source; how facts are emphasized or ignored; whose sense of "normal" is evident in the description or recreation of events; whose perception of time and of pleasure or pain we are being offered (Saul, 1994, p. 7). In so doing, we can call attention to issues that have affected (and continue to affect) the contemporary populace.

Connections to Curricular Issues

In *Information Power: Building Partnerships for Learning* (1998), the American Library Association reminds us that students integrate new information into their current knowledge, drawing conclusions by developing new ideas based on information they gather and connecting new ideas with prior knowledge (p. 19). A well-written, well-presented nonfiction work can assist in both stimulating interest in a previously unexplored area of study and enhancing preexisting knowledge. The Orbis Pictus Award Committee understands and appreciates the need for the continued support and strengthening of the school curriculum. It understands the powerful effect that materials available to young people can have on their learning. In this regard, we must consider the depth of knowledge apparent in a submitted work. We ask ourselves, Does this text add significantly to the body of literature already available on the topic? Does it "say (or illustrate) better" what we already have at hand? Is this a pioneering work on a subject about which nothing previously has been written for young people?

Dennis Fradin's *"We Have Conquered Pain": The Discovery of Anesthesia* (1996) is a case in point. During an age when technology has increased the type and number of surgical procedures, there is always concern about patient preparation and comfort level. Fradin's book offers a fascinating look at the origins of anesthesia and demonstrates to young people just how far we have come in addressing the need to reduce pain during invasive procedures. This work also serves as a reminder to young people of the importance of the process of discovery in science, a factor all too often not fully appreciated by the young. Fradin highlights process in an engaging manner. He also shares fascinating insights on the influence that rivalries among scientists had on the development of anesthesia.

The study of weather is an important component of the science curriculum. The impact of El Niño and other recently publicized environmental phenomena is under constant scrutiny in the news and consequently in classrooms around the country. As a result of weather changes due to global warming, the world has experienced an increased frequency of violent storms. Therefore, Patricia Lauber's book *Hurricanes: Earth's Mightiest Storms* (1996), with its clear discussions of the forecasting capabilities of meteorologists and the potential for economic and social devastation caused by these storms, as well as the accompanying brilliant photographs of hurricanes, is a strong contributor to the body of knowledge available for young people on the subject.

Diane Swanson's *Safari beneath the Sea: The Wonder World of the North Pacific Coast* (1994), winner of the Orbis Pictus Award for 1995, uses an engaging style to encourage interest in the deep waters of the North Pacific Coast. Swanson begins one chapter by stating, "Fish may not smell good but they certainly smell well" (p. 35). One can imagine a young reader reacting in amazement to the implications of this statement: "How can you breathe and smell through water?" Readers would certainly be fascinated by this "hook" and moved to keep reading. Swanson has an outstanding ability to reach young people through clearly explicated text and magnificently photographed examples of deepwater life.

Orbis Pictus Award selections have been particularly strong in the genre of biography, which transcends subject-area designation. Students are often asked to conduct research on specific individuals. Therefore, it is important to provide books that offer new information about well-known people, as well as information about those who were previously, sometimes purposely, overlooked. Speaking of informational picture books, Patricia J. Cianciolo, author of *Informational Picture Books for Children* (2000), reiterates the need for nonfiction for young people that avoids romanticizing and fictionalizing (p. 21). Romanticized and fictionalized offerings do not make significant contributions to the field and in fact can be perceived as devaluing the capabilities of young people. Cianciolo acknowledges that the subject matter of a book such as Diane Stanley's *Leonardo da Vinci* (1996), the 1997 Orbis Pictus Award winner, is not for everyone because of the specificity of its subject matter: "I have little doubt it is one that will be enjoyed and appreciated and probably long remembered by those readers who are already interested in visual art or the 'great masters' or by those who are 'ready' for this kind of literature and need only that extra little nudge to be connected with it" (p. 23). She goes on to describe the attributes of Stanley's presentation and comments on issues the Orbis Pictus Award Committee also felt helped make this work so significant that it deserved to be honored as the Orbis Pictus Award winner for 1997:

> Stanley's carefully written text details, but not too overwhelmingly for young readers, major aspects of da Vinci's successes and failures. His diverse talents as well as his human weaknesses are described. She makes quite clear his place in the history of art in general and his status and artistic accomplishments in relation to other noted artists of his time. Stanley's full-color, full-page paintings competently support and extend and make so much more concrete the specific paintings, frescoes, and sculptures discussed in the text. (Cianciolo, 2000, p. 23)

The committee has also found significance in works that, while they make an important contribution, may be controversial in their inclusion of subject matter deemed sensitive in educational contexts. Mary Pope Osborne, in her book *One World, Many Religions: The Ways We Worship* (1996), a 1997 Orbis Pictus honor book, effectively presents the topic of world religions not only from the perspective of the country of origin, but also through discussions of differences occurring when religions have been transplanted to other places and other cultures. For example, Buddhism is traced historically and explained from the point of view of its country of origin, India; however, Pope also contrasts Buddhism in India with Tibetan,

Zen, and Shin Buddhism. She explains the traditions and practices of Buddhism in present-day United States as well. Clearly, in a world of increased migration to places with different cultures and traditions, it is important to consider issues such as how religions are interpreted and practiced in different settings.

Conclusion

Books selected for the Orbis Pictus Award and for special recognition have the potential to enhance the knowledge base of young people. These books also offer them opportunities to think about issues and topics in new ways. The Orbis Pictus Award acknowledges nonfiction authors' outstanding contributions and highlights books that encourage young readers to take a look at works offering unique and noteworthy presentations on topics of significance.

References

American Association of School Librarians, American Library Association. (1998). *Information power: Building partnerships for learning.* Chicago: American Association of School Librarians, American Library Association.

Cianciolo, P. J. (2000). *Informational picture books for children.* Chicago: American Library Association.

Saul, E. W. (Ed). (1994). *Nonfiction for the classroom: Milton Meltzer on writing, history and social responsibility.* New York: Teachers College Press.

Children's Books

Aliki. (1999). *William Shakespeare & the Globe.* New York: HarperCollins.

Armstrong, J. (1998). *Shipwreck at the bottom of the world: The extraordinary true story of Shackleton and the* Endurance. New York: Crown.

Blumberg, Rhoda. (1996). *Full steam ahead: The race to build the transcontinental railroad.* Washington, DC: National Geographic Society.

Fradin, D. (1996). *"We have conquered pain": The discovery of anesthesia.* New York: McElderry/Simon & Schuster.

Freedman, R. (1996). *The life and death of Crazy Horse.* New York: Holiday House.

Haskins, J., & Benson, K. (1999). *Bound for America: The forced migration of Africans to the New World.* Illus. Floyd Cooper. New York: Lothrop, Lee and Shepard Books.

Lankford, M.D. (1996). *Jacks around the world.* New York: Morrow Junior Books.

Lauber, P. (1996). *Hurricanes: Earth's mightiest storms.* New York: Scholastic.

Murphy, J. (1993). *Across America on an emigrant train.* New York: Clarion Books.

Murphy, J. (1995). *The great fire*. New York: Scholastic.

Myers, W. D. (1999). *At her majesty's request: An African princess in Victorian England*. New York: Scholastic.

Osborne, M. P. (1996). *One world, many religions: The ways we worship*. New York: Knopf.

Stanley, D. (1996). *Leonardo da Vinci*. New York: Morrow Junior Books.

Stanley, J. (1992). *Children of the dust bowl: The true story of the school at Weedpatch Camp*. New York: Crown.

Swanson, D. (1994). *Safari beneath the sea: The wonder world of the North Pacific coast*. San Francisco: Sierra Club Books for Children.

II Award-Winning Authors Discuss Their Work

Edited by Richard M. Kerper

During the last decade, many changes have occurred in the writing of nonfiction and yet much has remained the same. In this section, nine writers of nonfiction for children—Rhoda Blumberg, Jennifer Owings Dewey, Jean Fritz, James Cross Giblin, Patricia Lauber, Jim Murphy, Mary Pope Osborne, Laurence Pringle, and Diane Swanson—reflect on their work and the publishing of nonfiction during the 1990s. They explore the forces that fuel their creativity and the issues that put a damper on their enthusiasm while reminiscing about books they published during the period.

- Diane Swanson reveals the influences that book selection processes in schools, book awards, and publishing trends have on a nonfiction writer's work.

- Laurence Pringle discusses the influence of the marketplace on his writing, the impact of adopting a narrative style, and concerns about accuracy—in this case, avoiding anthropomorphism.

- James Cross Giblin challenges the prescripts of editors and critics regarding the form of a nonfiction book and shares the influences that shaped his recent works.

- Patricia Lauber shows how the relaxation of publisher prescripts has permitted her to integrate science with other disciplines. She also notes the central role that illustrations play in her books.

- Rhoda Blumberg reflects on the need to lure digital-age readers into books with well-researched information and illustrations, carefully selected phrases that create mental images, and politically correct language and socially diverse topics that will speak to young people.

- Jennifer Owings Dewey provides a personal look at the evolution of her writing—from a desire to present the lives of animals untouched by human beings, to a desire to show the connection between human activity and wildlife.

- Mary Pope Osborne discloses her concerns and decisions in creating her 1996 book *One World, Many Religions,* which is on a subject rarely explored in children's nonfiction.
- Jean Fritz reveals her need to immerse herself in the world of her biographical subject in order to breathe life into her writing.
- Jim Murphy explores his research, writing, and publishing experiences and exposes his concerns about style and accuracy.

The experiences of these nine writers demonstrate both the stability and the change in nonfiction publishing for children and suggest issues that writers might face during the next decade.

6 A Wish for a New Century

Diane Swanson

When I first started writing for publication, I was a young mom with two small children, and I found myself seeing the world through their eyes. Typical kids, they took the time to check out a raindrop, to marvel at a worm, to imitate a chickadee. And they shared their enormous enthusiasm with me. Rachel Carson really knew what she was talking about when she wrote, "A child's world is fresh and new and beautiful, full of wonder and excitement" (Carson, 1965, p. 42).

Carson also wrote about her very special wish that every child could have a sense of wonder "so indestructible that it would last throughout life, as an unfailing antidote against the boredom and disenchantments of later years" (Carson, 1965, p. 43). That wish has influenced my books a great deal. In choosing to write children's nonfiction about nature, I have tried, in some small way, to cultivate readers' natural sense of wonder, to help it grow so strong that it might last a lifetime.

I think that's really what most writers of nonfiction are trying to do, whether they're writing about science, biography, sports, history, or the social issues of the day. Children's book expert Jo Carr wrote that the nonfiction author "proceeds from intellectual mastery of the subject to conviction and enthusiasm. . . . This kind of keen enthusiasm, passion if you will, is then transformed through imagination until the reader's passion is awakened in response" (Carr, 1982, p. 5). That passion is what helps to make a sense of wonder "indestructible" and a book memorable.

Throughout the last decade, nonfiction has been earning a stronger place in the world of children's literature. Overall, the quality of writing, illustration, and design has reached a greater level of excellence than before. Children's literature specialist Susan Hepler wrote, "For years nonfiction titles were viewed as the fusty and lackluster cousins of fiction. Now, these books look and read better than ever" (Hepler, 1998, p. 4). Far from being mere "collections of fact," they have been contributing to the growing body of "literature of fact."

But I don't think literature of fact for children is given its due. I still find teachers and librarians who purchase nonfiction books solely on the basis of their fit with school curricula. They seldom read these books before ordering them, or after, for that matter. And they rarely encourage children to read them for pleasure—nor do most parents.

On a personal level, I know people who suspect that I must really be a closet fiction writer. They ask sincerely, if not unkindly, "Wouldn't you rather be writing stories?" How do I convince them that I am thrilled to be telling stories about nature in its nonfictionalized form? Is there not a great, natural adventure in the exploration of the dark seas, five kilometers deep? In scientists who fly across vast, empty stretches of the sea floor in a submersible, then suddenly encounter a field splattered with red, yellow, and green? In discovering tall smokers that jet hot water rich with minerals? Scientists have even found gold here, something they had once thought only built up on land. Now they are finding new ocean life, giant clams and ghostly white crabs, thriving at these magical deep-sea vents. Nature is a never-ending, always unfolding mystery that is my great pleasure to research and share with young readers.

In this twenty-first century, it's obvious that authors of nonfiction for children have a long way to go to convince the adult public, the people who select books for kids, that our genre is a worthy read. So it's fortunate that we have, as allies in this cause, organizations that sponsor awards for excellence in writing kids' nonfiction. Not only do these organizations stimulate further work in this genre, but they also encourage the public to read it by highlighting books of quality and heaping them with praise.

Compared to the number of awards that recognize children's fiction, tributes specifically to nonfiction are few and far between. That makes them all the more important. These include, among others, the Orbis Pictus Award for Outstanding Nonfiction for Children, which has been given annually by the National Council of Teachers of English throughout the last decade. Since the late 1980s, the Information Book Award has been presented each year by the Canadian Children's Literature Roundtables. And in November 1999, the first ever Norma Fleck Award, a $10,000 prize, was given in Canada to honor children's nonfiction. It was established in memory of Norma Fleck, a woman who believed that quality reading enriches one's life.

Having received the Orbis Pictus Award and having had five books shortlisted for the Information Book Award, I can personally attest to the value of tributes in encouraging the writing of nonfiction. That recognition has given me the confidence to continue and encouraged me to extend the range of nature topics I choose for my books. It has also opened up new opportunities for me. As well as continuing to write for the eight- to twelve-year-old set, I also have been developing a number of books for five- to seven-year-olds. Soon I will be adding books for preschoolers to the list. It's a great feeling to be reaching out to children of all ages.

At the same time, I have some concerns about how this past decade has affected my writing and the work of other nonfiction writers for children. The rising costs of publishing and its dwindling returns have been forcing trade book publishers, more than ever, to develop books for the largest possible market. As a result, they are printing fewer books that have a regional focus or specialized topics. During the last five years, I have seen the focus of my own work move from regional, to national, to continental, to global. One publisher recently commented that books today have to be in "nowhereland" to sell internationally. While that works for the treatment of some subjects, I think it's important to be able to introduce children to a smaller slice of the pie—the wonders of their own regions, of their own backyards.

Another concern I share with other authors is the shorter length of children's nonfiction books, both in number of pages and number of words. Science writer Dorothy Hinshaw Patent pointed out that her first book, published in 1973 for readers ages eight to twelve, contained ninety-five pages and many full-text pages of about 390 words. A book she wrote in 1997 for the same age group contained sixty-nine pages and few full-text pages of about 290 words (Patent, 1998, 311–12). While Patent found a way to treat her subject well, the trend toward slimmer books with fewer words often forces writers to make tough choices. Sometimes they offer a superficial treatment of a subject, or they narrow the scope of a topic instead of giving it the treatment it merits. Young readers deserve better.

My wish for this new century of ours is that we as authors have the opportunity to produce children's nonfiction that is like a child's world: "fresh and new and beautiful, full of wonder and excitement." Rachel Carson would wish that too.

References

Carr, J. (1982). *Beyond fact: Nonfiction for children and young people*. Chicago: American Library Association.

Carson, R. (1965). *The sense of wonder*. New York: Harper & Row.

Hepler, S. (1998). Nonfiction books for children: New directions, new challenges. In R. A. Bamford & J. V. Kristo (Eds.), *Making facts come alive: Choosing quality nonfiction literature K–8* (pp. 3–17). Norwood, MA: Christopher-Gordon.

Patent, D. H. (1998). Science books for children: An endangered species? *Horn Book Magazine* (May/June): 309–14.

Lessons Learned from a Butterfly

Laurence Pringle

In 1966 I wrote in my diary, "In the eve, finished editing and typing dinosaur book. At long last, ready to send it off—what a relief!" Those last words were the understatement of that year, and it was only March 11.

That manuscript was my first attempt at a book and the longest piece of writing I had ever faced. The writing had dragged on for months; it was homework after my magazine editing job and my putting-the-kids-to-bed "job." It had been such an ordeal that if there had been more space in the diary, I would have added, "Even if this is published I will NEVER try to write another book!"

It is amusing to recall those 1966 words as I turn at my desk and look at that first book—published in 1968—lined up with eighty-nine of my other titles on nearby shelves. Looking at the spines of ninety books that span more than three decades, I notice something else. Beginning in the mid-1980s and continuing through the 1990s, the jacket spines are more colorful. If you pluck from the shelf almost any of my books of the 1990s, its jacket and the pages within are more appealing—in design and in color—than most books published before 1985.

It was about then that publishers recognized that the children who were potential readers had grown accustomed to full color in magazines, films, video games, and television. Another factor also affected publishers of children's books in the mid- to late 1980s: the policies of the Reagan-Bush presidencies reduced federal funds for school libraries. With this institutional market reduced, many publishers looked to the bookstore market, where appearances matter a lot. Greater emphasis was placed on the design of children's books and on liberal use of color—a breakthrough in nonfiction. Often, to make full use of art or photos, the amount of text was reduced.

The new nonfiction books look terrific, but some of them remind me of people we all encounter in life—utterly charming but lacking in substance. Many young readers discover that there isn't much within some great looking books. These books may meet the needs of reluctant readers, or others who have stunted attention spans, but not those of children and teenagers who are hungry for more than cursory knowledge of a subject.

In the 1990s, publishers also targeted younger readers because of a "baby boom" bulge in the population. This, coupled with the declining school library market, caused many publishers to lose interest in young adult (YA) nonfiction, which had been a major part of my work. Through the years, I had written about a dozen YA books for Macmillan on environmental problems, with a scattering of such titles for other publishers. These books explored the science, technology, and sociopolitical aspects of natural resources issues, earned good reviews, and usually sold at least 12,000 copies. (One of the last to go out of print was *Rain of Troubles: The Science and Politics of Acid Rain* [1988].)

Sales in those numbers were not enough, it seemed, in the 1990s. Publisher after publisher said "no" to proposals for similar projects. "Write younger, write shorter" was the rule, which, fortunately, I had also been doing for decades. Still, I miss the opportunity to go into more depth on the complexity of a subject in a YA book of 124 pages. An environmental issue can be dealt with fairly and effectively in a 64-page book, but a longer treatment is ideal. Presenting it in a 48-page book is also possible but increases the risk of oversimplifying, of omitting important ideas. This is not true when the subject matter is, say, dinosaurs, but certainly is true when the subject is, say, global warming. Understanding that issue involves not just the science but also knowing something about international politics and the efforts of some of the most powerful industries on Earth to deny that there is a problem.

The 1990s did offer me writing opportunities I had never dreamed of: a G-rated autobiography, *Nature! Wild and Wonderful* (1997d), in the Meet the Author series, and *One Room School* (1998). What a wonderful surprise, to discover that attending a one-room school, which seemed so ordinary and unremarkable to me as a child, would become a fascinating experience to others at the turn of the century.

Through the years, I've been too busy writing to study children's nonfiction literature or to plot a career path. I attempted picture book fiction (most recently *Naming the Cat* [1997c]) simply because reading such books to my young children was such a delight for us all. Mostly I wrote more nonfiction of the sort that had been successful in the past. Then, in 1993, editor Harold Underdown urged me to think of writing narrative nonfiction.

Belatedly I realized that I had been using story in my nonfiction from the very beginning. In my first book, *Dinosaurs and Their World* (1968), the chapter "The Puzzle of the Duckbills" is a bit like a mystery, tracing investigations by scientists of the crests on the heads of this group of dinosaurs. The book *Death Is Natural* (1977) introduces a "character," a rabbit, who quickly dies, but readers then follow some of the elements within the rabbit's body to a surprising destination. In many books, I have also followed the stories of scientific investigation and of legislative battles. In some—most recently *Elephant Woman: Cynthia Moss Explores the World of Elephants* (1997a)—the "character" is a real person who readers first meet as a child, then follow into adulthood and an unusual career.

In May 1993, Harold Underdown, then at Orchard Books, spoke admiringly of the books of Holling Clancy Holling, especially *Minn of the Mississippi* (1951). This book is about the life of a snapping turtle but is rich with connections to other life, history, geography, geology, etc. We talked about creating a somewhat simpler 64-page book with those same qualities. This conversation led to the creation of *An Extraordinary Life: The Story of a Monarch Butterfly* (1997b).

For several days, I thought about birds, whales, and other creatures that make epic journeys. I dismissed monarch butterflies because of several recent titles on that subject, but I kept coming back to them. Something felt right about monarchs. This book, if I could write it as Harold and I envisioned it, would be different from all of the others.

As I learned more and more from monarch researchers, the details of one butterfly's life fell into a four-chapter outline that formed a sentence: "From a Massachusetts hayfield, across a continent, to a mountain in Mexico—an extraordinary life." Western Massachusetts seemed a logical place to begin because it was the home of Fred Morrison, a prime source of information, and of Bob Marstall, who would illustrate the book.

Writing about the life of Danaus the monarch, I was happy to include a few of my own observations. My Siamese cat sometimes ambushed butterflies in the flower garden, and I had seen migrating monarchs dip down to investigate bright orange plastic cones at my kids' soccer practices. I used both incidents in Danaus's journey. Most of the information, of course, came from scientific journals and books, and from the scientists themselves.

By coincidence, as I wrote about Danaus in 1994, I read the words of E. B. White responding to questions about *Charlotte's Web* (1952). He said that animals were part of his world, and he tried to present them faithfully and with respect. He had spent many hours observing the behavior of an orb web-spinning spider and also learned what scientists knew about them. Aside from speaking, spelling "TERRIFIC" in her web, expressing human emotion, and so on, Charlotte acts just as a spider really acts in nature.

Though writing nonfiction, I wanted readers to care about the female monarch butterfly in my book—without the aid of anthropomorphism. I was particularly cautious about implying that she was thinking when I referred to butterfly wisdom stored in her ganglion. I deliberately wrote, "Without thought, without practice, Danaus gave her wings a powerful downstroke" (Pringle, 1997b, p. 20) when she first took flight. And later, "the nerve cells in her ganglion were much too simple for her to think about how she was leaving her winter home or to feel regret about leaving forever the special environment of the mountain fir forests" (p. 53).

Reading that sentence long after the book was published, I realize it accomplishes two things. It stresses that the butterfly does not have human emotions, while at the same time encouraging feelings *for her* in readers—a neat trick that I performed unintentionally.

After arriving in Mexico, Danaus "looked as fit and pretty as the day she first took flight" (p. 41), I wrote. An editor at Orchard (one who followed Harold Underdown and preceded Melanie Kroupa, who was the book's final and actual editor) thought that line was anthropomorphic. I disagreed. The words did not say Danaus "felt" fit and pretty; they just described her. The sentence stayed.

The manuscript of *An Extraordinary Life* was read by Dr. Lincoln Brower, then of the University of Florida and the world's leading authority on monarchs. He pointed out a few borderline anthropomorphic words that I then changed, corrected factual errors, and directed me to other researchers who specialized in certain aspects of monarch life. In response to some questions, he just said, "We don't know."

Despite my vigilance, Patricia Manning, reviewing the book for *School Library Journal,* did find "a modicum of anthropomorphism" that she described as "infrequent and low key" (Manning, 1997, p. 150). She cited use of the word *frantic,* as in "Danaus became almost frantic with her desire to find the milkweed her young would need to eat" (Pringle, 1997b, p. 55). She's right; I could have reworked that sentence to say that Danaus "looked frantic."

Rereading the book carefully, I found two other instances where I may have strayed too close to anthropomorphism. Danaus had arrived in the Mexican mountains, and I wrote, "Danaus must have felt at home" (p. 40). I then referred to the information in her ganglion, passed down from generations of monarchs, which had guided her to that place. That information enabled her to sense that she had reached the right place, a better way to put it. Later in that chapter, Danaus escaped being eaten by an oriole. Concluding the incident, I wrote a sentence that seems to imply she learned from the experience and chose a safer place to rest. This suggests something about butterfly behavior that may not be true.

I regret unintentionally giving Danaus human qualities since the "infrequent and low key" instances could have been easily fixed, and Danaus would have remained a character whom readers can care about. She is not Charlotte, she's just a butterfly, but some readers have told me they are in tears at the end of the book.

The success of *An Extraordinary Life* led me to write more narrative nonfiction, notably *A Dragon in the Sky: The Story of a Green Darner Dragonfly* (2001), also illustrated by Bob Marstall. I learned a few lessons from writing about Danaus the monarch that I applied to Anax the green darner. Of course, a fierce predatory dragonfly is not as endearing as a butterfly, but readers will find Anax treated faithfully and with respect as he zooms, hovers, swoops, and sets out on a remarkable journey.

References

Holling, H. C. (1951). *Minn of the Mississippi*. Boston: Houghton Mifflin.

Manning, P. Review of *An Extraordinary Life* by Laurence Pringle. *School Library Journal 43* (1997): 149–50.

Pringle, L. (1968). *Dinosaurs and Their World*. New York: Harcourt.

Pringle, L. (1977). *Death Is Natural*. New York: Four Winds Press.

Pringle, L. (1988). *Rain of Troubles: The Science and Politics of Acid Rain*. New York: Macmillan.

Pringle, L. (1997a). *Elephant Woman: Cynthia Moss Explores the World of Elephants*. New York: Atheneum.

Pringle, L. (1997b). *An Extraordinary Life: The Story of a Monarch Butterfly*. New York: Orchard Books.

Pringle, L. (1997c). *Naming the Cat*. New York: Walker.

Pringle, L. (1997d). *Nature! Wild and Wonderful*. Katonah, New York: Richard C. Owen.

Pringle, L. (1998). *One Room School*. Honesdale, PA: Boyds Mills Press.

Pringle, L. (2001). *A Dragon in the Sky: The Story of a Green Darner Dragonfly*. New York: Orchard Books.

White, E. B. (1952). *Charlotte's Web*. New York: Harper.

8 Presidents, Plagues, and a Pilot: My Writing Life in the 1990s

James Cross Giblin

The last decade of the twentieth century began with a major change in my professional life. In January 1990, I took early retirement as editor-in-chief of Clarion Books, a position I had held for twenty-two years. For more than ten of those years, I had fulfilled my editorial responsibilities while writing a growing number of nonfiction books for young people. With each book, I longed more and more to put my writing in first place. Now at last I was going to do it.

I didn't give up editing entirely, however. The stimulating exchanges I had enjoyed with my authors were too meaningful to abandon. And so I continued to edit eight or ten writers including Eve Bunting, Mary Downing Hahn, Eileen Christelow, and Marion Dane Bauer. Maintaining a creative relationship with these people was gratifying on many levels, but I must confess there were times when I was in the final stages of writing a book that I resented having to set it aside and edit someone else's manuscript. On balance, though, the gratification far outweighed any resentment I may have felt.

In the 1980s, several books I wrote on offbeat topics—*Chimney Sweeps: Yesterday and Today* (1982), *From Hand to Mouth: Or, How We Invented Knives, Forks, Spoons, and Chopsticks & the Table Manners to Go with Them* (1987), and *Let There Be Light: A Book about Windows* (1988)—had helped to establish my reputation. Now, at the start of the 1990s, I feared I was getting into a rut and thought a change of pace might be in order. This feeling was reinforced when a well-known children's librarian came up to me at a gathering and said in all seriousness, "I just loved your book about windows and I have the perfect idea for a follow-up—doors!"

Dismayed by comments like that—What would follow doors? Ceilings? Floors?—I decided it was definitely time to try something new. But first I had to fulfill two holdover contracts from the 1980s, *The Truth about Unicorns* (1991b) and *Be Seated: A Book about Chairs* (1993). Along with work on these topics, I began the journey into new territory. At the suggestion of an editor I knew at Scholastic, Dianne Hess, I tried my hand at a biography for seven- to nine-year-olds, *George Washington* (1992b). I followed it up with a longer biography for eight- to twelve-year-olds, *Edith Wilson: The Woman Who Ran the United States* (1992a), and another biography for the seven to nine age group, *Thomas Jefferson* (1994).

The Washington and Jefferson books challenged me in several ways. Not only were they among my first attempts at biography, but they were also the first books I had written for younger children. I enjoyed discovering little-known facts about the two men and then seeking ways to express them simply without becoming simplistic. It was also great fun to see how the illustrator, Michael Dooling, interpreted my texts in his dramatic oil paintings. I shared some of my research with him—brochures about Mount Vernon and Monticello, notes I had made on tours of both sites, etc.—but we never met in person. This is par for the course with picture book authors and illustrators; they usually communicate via the book's editor, who can resolve any conflicts that may develop.

The biography of Edith Wilson, published in a series about Women of Our Time, proved to be a less happy experience. I knew from the start that series publication has its advantages and disadvantages. On the one hand, you get a certain amount of marketing and promotional support just from being part of a known series. But an author has to face the fact that series books rarely receive the same amount of critical attention that individual titles do.

Beyond that, the Women of Our Time series had other drawbacks that I failed to notice sufficiently at the outset. By the early 1990s, when *Edith Wilson* was published, the standards and expectations for juvenile biographies, and children's nonfiction generally, had changed drastically from those prevailing in earlier decades. Whereas a certain amount of fictionalization in biographies had once been acceptable, reviewers, librarians, and teachers now demanded strict accuracy bolstered by extensive source notes. Many nonfiction books of the past had been illustrated with black-and-white drawings, but most nonfiction books of the 1990s were illustrated solely with photographs, some of them in color. And every nonfiction book, even those for the picture book age, now included an index.

The Women of Our Time series didn't fall into the trap of fictionalization, but on every other count the titles in it employed an outdated approach. In an attempt to make them resemble junior novels and thus attract readers who might not like nonfiction, the books were illustrated with drawings, even when—as in the case of *Edith Wilson*—excellent photographs were readily available. There was a page at the back of the books for an Author's Note, but no space was allowed for source notes. There wasn't even room for an index!

I was so eager to write a biography of Edith Wilson for older readers that I overlooked these drawbacks while I was working on the manuscript. But I became sharply aware of them as the book went through production, and pleaded—unsuccessfully—for at least a one-page index to be included. Given my concerns, the book received a warmer reception than I had anticipated. It got some good reviews—although several noted the lack of an index and source notes—and was chosen as a selection by a hardcover children's book club. More important, doing it gave me the confidence to undertake more ambitious biographies in the future.

Several things that happened to and around me in the early 1990s had a profound effect on my writing. Some were extremely positive, such as the purchase of a two-bedroom apartment in the fall of 1992. For thirteen years I'd lived in an alcove studio apartment in the same high-rise building. The studio suited my purposes as long as I went out to work at Clarion five days a week, but once I started spending most of my time at home, the single, large room began to seem terribly cramped.

Now, in the new apartment on the sixteenth floor, I had a separate home office for the first time—and a corner one, to boot. There was room in it for a computer, which I learned to master with the help of a skillful tutor. And through the windows, when I took the time to look out, there were marvelous city views to the north and west. Living and working in the new apartment gave me a feeling of expansiveness that I think is reflected in the books I wrote later in the 1990s.

Another event that cheered me was the election of Bill Clinton as president in November 1992. In a curious bit of timing, the closing on my apartment occurred the day after the election, when the final returns were still coming in. With Clinton, I felt for the first time since the 1970s that an administration was in power in Washington that shared my views on education, reading, and the arts. Some major disappointments came later—especially after the Republican Right gained control of the House in 1994. But I continued to believe that the country was far better off under a Clinton administration than it would have been had George Bush been reelected, to be succeeded perhaps by Dan Quayle.

Other events in the early 1990s had a destructive effect on me—at least at first. In December 1991, I headed toward my seat on the dais at a Clarion sales conference, failed to see that there was a sizable gap between the raised platform and the back wall of the meeting room, and stepped off into space. When I came to a moment later, I was lying on my back on the floor, and when I stood up pain shot through my left foot. Fortunately I hadn't broken anything, but X rays revealed that the fall had torn a ligament and large amounts of soft tissue. My podiatrist told me these injuries would probably take longer to heal than a break, and he was right. It was almost two months before I walked without a cane, and six months before the foot began to feel normal again. To this day it starts to ache if I stand in one position too long.

While the injury was in no way life threatening, the long recuperation process made me appreciate simple, everyday things I'd taken for granted, such as walking to the post office in the next block. It also prodded me into tackling a project that I'd been contemplating for almost ten years but held back from committing myself to because I knew how demanding it would be. This was the book that grew into *When Plague Strikes* (1995), a comparative study of three epidemic diseases, the Black Death, smallpox, and AIDS.

I never know exactly why I want to write a book until I get well into it, and that was certainly true of *When Plague Strikes*. Oh, I thought kids would relish the gory details of the Black Death, and that epidemic seemed like a good parallel to the deadly contemporary plague, AIDS. To flesh out the book, I decided to cover a third disease, and after considering several others—tuberculosis, cholera, influenza, etc.—I settled on smallpox. I felt it would provide the best balance to the Black Death and AIDS because smallpox is the only epidemic disease so far that's been completely conquered.

That was the thought process, based on my knowledge of the market and audience, that I went through in planning *When Plague Strikes*. But it wasn't until I got into the research for the AIDS section that I discovered the emotional reasons that motivated me to write the book. Thousands of people in the 1980s had been affected by AIDS, many of them fatally. Among the dead were some of the most gifted creators of children's books, including two young men I'd worked with, the novelist Gary W. Bargar and the picture book author-illustrator Ron Wegen. I realized that *When Plague Strikes* was my way of dealing with those losses and paying tribute to all the talented people whose lives had been cut short so tragically. When the manuscript was finished, I dedicated it to the memory of Gary and Ron.

Because it told three separate stories, *When Plague Strikes* took longer to research and write than any of my previous books. I began in-depth research for it in January 1993, started writing the Black Death section in June of that year while still researching smallpox and AIDS, and finally broke through to the end of the book a year later in June 1994. As I was racing to finish it (I had already missed several deadlines and was determined not to miss another), I came down with what I thought was a bad case of the flu but turned out to be walking pneumonia. Writing *When Plague Strikes* had literally made me sick!

The only treatment for the viral disease was rest, which I very much needed. Fortunately, my editor didn't think the manuscript required much in the way of revision, just some tightening and clarification here and there. But I still had to decide how the book would be illustrated.

On most of my other nonfiction books, I'd been responsible for gathering the photographs and prints to be used as illustrations, and the same was true of my contract for *When Plague Strikes*. But the more I thought about it, the more I concluded that a mix of photographs and prints would be wrong for this book. Few artists had attempted to portray the ravages of the Black Death; for smallpox I might be able to find portraits of people such as Edward Jenner and photographs of the disease's victims; and of course there were countless photographs of those involved in the AIDS crisis. But would this mix of illustrations result in a visually unified book? I doubted it.

I expressed these concerns to my editor, Toni Markiet, and together we decided that the best solution would be to get an artist who could do a strong jacket design and an introductory illustration for each of the three sections. But who? We went back and forth, discussing various possibilities, and then we both hit on the same name: David Frampton. Known for his powerful woodcuts, he seemed the perfect choice for the assignment. But would he want to take it on? Toni sent him a copy of the manuscript and got a quick response. He would love to illustrate the book and already had an idea for the jacket.

Frampton did a wonderful job, and I'm sure his woodcuts contributed greatly to the impression *When Plague Strikes* made on reviewers and readers. But in its design, as in its writing, the book quietly ignored the widely accepted 1990s recipe for successful children's nonfiction publishing. Conventional wisdom had it that texts for all age groups should be as succinct as possible, and should be broken up with a generously scaled illustration—preferably a photograph—on almost every page. *When Plague Strikes* had a lengthy, complex text and no interior illustrations at all except for a frontispiece woodcut opposite the title page and a double-page woodcut to introduce each of the book's three parts. Yet no one dismissed it as boring or old-fashioned. Quite the contrary.

This taught me an important lesson that I have tried to apply to the books I've written since *When Plague Strikes*. Don't pay too much attention to what others say about how a nonfiction book should be written or what it should look like. Let the content determine the form; if it requires a large number of illustrations, do all you can to get them. But if it doesn't, don't be afraid to let the text stand on its own.

After completing *When Plague Strikes*, I plunged immediately into the research for another "big" book: *Charles A. Lindbergh: A Human Hero* (1997). Lindbergh intrigued me as a subject because of the many lives he led. First there was the young pilot, idolized the world over after his pathbreaking nonstop flight to Paris in 1927. Then there was the grief-stricken father, searching desperately for his kidnapped infant son while a nation looked on in horror and sorrow. Later there was the determined isolationist, speaking out against U.S. involvement in World War II even as many of his oldest friends turned against him. And finally there was the ardent conservationist of his last years, who said, "I would rather have birds than airplanes" (Giblin, 1997, p. 186).

What linked all these different aspects of Lindbergh, I asked myself. The book's subtitle, *A Human Hero,* indicates the answer I found. In a time when we tend to fall back on absolutes—something is all good or all bad—I wanted to show young people that a person can be a hero in one context, as Lindbergh was when he flew to Paris, and a villain in another, as Lindbergh appeared to many people when he blamed influential Jews in the media and elsewhere for pushing the United States toward war. Moreover, the same characteristics may underlie both the person's heroism and his villainy. In Lindbergh's case, it was his stubbornness that made him persist in his plan to fly to Paris no matter how many obstacles blocked his path. And it was that same stubbornness that made him hold fast to his isolationist stand no matter what arguments his friends raised against it.

As I got deeper into the book, I discovered that I had a personal reason, too, for wanting to write about Lindbergh. While he and I couldn't have been more unalike in many ways—from his earliest youth he had been something of a daredevil, whereas I have always been cautious physically—in others we were remarkably similar. We were both only children, the sons of lawyer fathers and independent, well-educated mothers who had been teachers. And we both had a reputation for being "loners," individuals who weren't afraid to embark on new ventures all by ourselves. I'm convinced these similarities helped me get a firmer grasp on Lindbergh's personality as I recounted the important events in his life. By the time I finished the manuscript, they had also helped me gain a better understanding of myself.

The Lindbergh biography took even longer to research and write than *When Plague Strikes*. I began the research for it in August 1994, started writing the manuscript in January 1995, and completed it in August 1996. It was also my longest manuscript to date, coming in at just over two hundred pages. I feared my editor, Dorothy Briley, would ask me to cut it and I didn't see where I could. But Dorothy reassured me by saying, "It's long, yes, but everything in it seems necessary. I think we should go with it the way it is." And so we did.

Once the text was resolved, I focused on the picture research. There was never any doubt that the book would be illustrated with black-and-white photographs; the only question was how many there would be room for. We ended up including seventy-two, and I was particularly pleased with some that, to my knowledge, had never appeared in any previous books about Lindbergh. Several came from the family photo albums of his boyhood and youth that he'd left to the Minnesota Historical Society and that I discovered on a research trip to St. Paul. Others, from the Missouri Historical Society, showed him in Nazi Germany in the 1930s, smiling up at his German hosts before taking off on a test flight in a new fighter plane.

Dorothy Briley spared no expense on the book's production. It was printed on an excellent grade of paper in a generous 7 1/2" x 10" format. Designer Carol Goldenberg chose a simple but elegant typeface for the text and scaled the photos so that they would make the strongest possible impact. We were also fortunate in getting the outstanding artist Barry Moser to do the jacket painting of a troubled-looking Lindbergh in his pilot's outfit.

This kind of painstaking attention to detail is essential if a nonfiction book is to receive the attention it deserves in today's highly competitive marketplace. And I can honestly say that I've never been as pleased with the overall effect of a book of mine as I was when Dorothy handed me one of the first bound copies of *Charles A. Lindbergh*. There was absolutely nothing about its physical production that I would have wanted changed. (That's not to say there weren't places in the text that I wished I could take another crack at. I've never been completely satisfied with any piece of writing I've done, and I don't expect I ever will be.)

Since *Lindbergh* I've written three other books and guest edited and introduced a fourth. *The Mystery of the Mammoth Bones* (1999) grew out of primary source material that fascinated me—the journals and diaries of the artist-scientist Charles Wilson Peale—and gave me a chance to write a nonfiction book structured like a detective story. *The Amazing Life of Benjamin Franklin* (2000a) rounded off the trio of biographies that had begun with *George Washington* and *Thomas Jefferson*, and enabled me to put to use what I'd learned about writing for a wide age span, from age seven up to twelve or thirteen. *Secrets of the Sphinx* (in press) took me back to ancient Egypt (I'd been there before with *The Riddle of the Rosetta Stone* [1990]) and provided the basis for another intriguing archaeological puzzle whose secrets have still not been completely revealed.

The anthology, *The Century That Was: Reflections on the Last One Hundred Years* (2000b), presented a fresh challenge that I was eager to take on for a number of reasons. The idea of doing a collection of original essays about American life in the twentieth century came from the publisher, Atheneum, but the choice of contributors and topics was left to me and Marcia Marshall, Atheneum's inhouse editor on the project. I was thrilled when such outstanding writers as Katherine Paterson, Russell Freedman, Walter Dean Myers, Lois Lowry, Jim Murphy, Eve Bunting, and Laurence Pringle said "yes" to our invitation to contribute. It was a pleasure working with them as an editor and then describing their combined efforts in my introduction. I felt as if my two professional identities, that of editor and of author, had been brought together in a new and satisfying way.

Early in this new century, I am troubled by several trends in children's book publishing that don't bode well for the writers of individual nonfiction books. Mergers and takeovers have wiped out a number of long-established imprints, such as Macmillan, Scribner's, and Morrow, that always included many nonfiction titles on their lists. The remaining trade publishers have been concentrating their efforts in recent years on reaching the bookstore market. They have issued more flashy picture books with bookstore appeal and fewer nonfiction books for older readers directed toward the so-called "institutional market" of school and public libraries.

Taking up the nonfiction slack have been the series publishers such as Enslow Books, Franklin Watts, and Millbrook Press. But authors of series books have to be prepared to accept certain limitations, as I indicated earlier. Their manuscripts must conform to a specified length in order to fit into the series format, and budgetary constraints frequently determine the number and type of illustrations included. Established writers who have been accustomed to more freedom in their work often find it difficult to adjust to these restrictions. But for many nonfiction writers, the choice is series publication or nothing as their former publishing outlets shift their focus or go out of business.

On my darker days, I sometimes wonder about the future of all nonfiction books, including the series titles. Will they be supplanted in time by the Internet and other electronic forms of information transmission? Will nonfiction writers be employed in the creation of Web sites instead of books? Then I remind myself that it doesn't pay to look too far ahead. If you do, you may fail to make the most of the project that's on your plate at the moment. For me, that's another "big" book in the vein of *When Plague Strikes* and the Lindbergh biography: *The Great Dictators*, a comparative biography of Adolf Hitler, Joseph Stalin, and Mao Zedong, the three dictators whose actions had an impact, direct or indirect, on almost everyone who lived in the twentieth century.

Once again I have a personal interest in exploring this material. When I was a young man, I was intrigued by social systems that differed from the one I'd always lived in. Wanting to see these societies for myself, I made two trips to the Soviet Union during the Khrushchev era in 1962 and 1964, and visited China in 1975, the last year of Mao's reign. Now, in writing about Hitler, Stalin, and Mao from an older, more experienced vantage point, I hope to gain a better understanding of why they did what they did—for myself first of all, and then for my young readers.

Ten years ago, just after I retired from Clarion, I wrote an autobiography for a reference book publisher. I ended it by saying that I was "excited and a bit apprehensive" as I embarked at age fifty-six on a new career as a freelance writer and editor. "However," I went on, "it's from such conflicting feelings that accomplishments often grow" (Giblin 1991a, p. 101). Now, ten years later, I can only echo those sentiments as I look ahead to this new century, this new millennium. I'm still excited and still apprehensive. But the books I've written in the 1990s gave me the courage to tackle challenging subject matter and the confidence to believe I can bring it off. And that's what I plan to continue doing in the years ahead.

References   Giblin, J. C. (1982). *Chimney sweeps: Yesterday and today.* New York: Crowell.

Giblin, J. C. (1987). *From hand to mouth: Or, how we invented knives, forks, spoons, and chopsticks & the table manners to go with them.* New York: Crowell.

Giblin, J. C. (1988). *Let there be light: A book about windows.* New York: Crowell.

Giblin, J. C. (1990). *The riddle of the Rosetta Stone.* New York: Crowell.

Giblin, J. C. (1991a). James Cross Giblin. In *Something about the Author Autobiography Series.* Vol. 12. Detroit: Gale Research.

Giblin, J. C. (1991b). *The truth about unicorns.* New York: HarperCollins.

Giblin, J. C. (1992a). *Edith Wilson: The woman who ran the United States.* New York: Viking.

Giblin, J. C. (1992b). *George Washington: A picture book biography*. New York: Scholastic.

Giblin, J. C. (1993). *Be seated: A book about chairs*. New York: HarperCollins.

Giblin, J. C. (1994). *Thomas Jefferson: A picture book biography*. New York: Scholastic, 1994.

Giblin, J. C. (1995). *When plague strikes: The Black Death, smallpox, AIDS*. New York: HarperCollins.

Giblin, J. C. (1997). *Charles A. Lindbergh: A human hero*. New York: Clarion Books.

Giblin, J. C. (1999). *The mystery of the mammoth bones, and how it was solved*. New York: HarperCollins.

Giblin, J. C. (2000a). *The amazing life of Benjamin Franklin*. New York: Scholastic.

Giblin, J. C. (Ed.). (2000b). *The century that was: Reflections on the last one hundred years*. New York: Atheneum.

Giblin, J. C. (in press). *Secrets of the Sphinx*. New York: Scholastic.

Giblin, J. C. (forthcoming). *The great dictators*. Unpublished manuscript.

Outside the Box

Patricia Lauber

T hinking outside the box" is a phrase I keep meeting as I read about companies or entrepreneurs trying to position themselves for the future in a sea of new technologies. I don't know where the phrase came from, but I like it because it's short, simple, to the point, and even graphic. In fact, I like it so much that I'm going to borrow it to characterize some of my own work over the past decade.

In my case, the "box" is the science book I have traditionally written. It is closely focused and has a subject that fills me with enthusiasm that I hope to pass on to young readers. It's as accurate and clear as I can make it. And it has a narrative thread that ties all the pieces together. My hope is to produce a book that will both inform and pleasure readers, and thus encourage scientific literacy.

My interest in promoting scientific literacy is closely allied with my ecological and environmental concerns. And so it was a small step to begin thinking that at least some of the science books I was writing could and should go beyond the boundaries of one branch of science and reach outside the box into other sciences and even other disciplines. With other books, I might start by thinking outside the box and then reach back in, using science to expand and elucidate nonscientific concepts. Either way, I could help readers see that science is not a thing apart but interwoven with many areas of our lives.

Hurricanes: Earth's Mightiest Storms (1996b) is a good example of reaching outside the box. A large part of the book is what one might expect in a book about hurricanes: graphic accounts of some big storms; how, where, and why hurricanes form; attempts to modify them; how they are studied and tracked. But there is much more to the story. Both demography and ecology are natural additions to the meteorology of a hurricane book.

Hurricanes occur in cycles of high or low frequency. A period when many big storms make a landfall on the East and Gulf Coasts is followed by years when almost no big storms come ashore. The United States recently experienced a low-frequency cycle that lasted

---

between twenty and thirty years. During this time, many people forgot about the danger of hurricanes; many were born and grew up without having experienced a hurricane. More and more people moved toward the shore. Today, 44 million people live along the coastline from Maine to Texas—in hurricane territory.

Where people move, cities grow; suburbs sprout; shopping malls spring up; retirement communities open; houses and other buildings, as well as trailer camps, cover land that was once open. In some areas, construction is shoddy and building inspection lax. Burgeoning population growth and unplanned coastal development combine to create a catastrophe waiting to happen.

If I were writing *Hurricanes* today, the book would tell of the painful lessons learned by the people of North Carolina during the 1999 hurricane season. The previous decade had brought the eastern part of the state a boom in population and an agricultural expansion that made North Carolina the second biggest producer of pork in the country. But the expansion took place on the coastal plain. In 1999 flooding triggered by heavy hurricane rains took lives and destroyed homes as rivers spilled over their banks and levees. It caused some four thousand huge lagoons of treated hog waste to overflow, and also drowned more than two million hogs, turkeys, and chickens. No one knows how long wells will be polluted or what the effect will be of all the waste matter that has flowed into Pimlico Sound, where fish from the waters of Long Island and Florida go to lay their eggs. North Carolina is rebuilding, but it is not putting things back the way they were.

A different sort of ecological problem arose in south Florida when Hurricane Andrew made a landfall in 1992 and cut a swath through Everglades National Park. This part of Florida has survived and recovered from many hurricanes. But by 1992, houses were crowding the edges of the park, and in their gardens homeowners had introduced certain imported plants, called exotics, that are fast growing and thrive in disturbed areas. Exotics soon began appearing in areas of the park damaged by Andrew. The danger was that they would take over and crowd out the slower-growing native species.

Does it matter? Very much! Green plants form the base of countless food chains in the park. Change the plants and you force a change in the kinds of animals that can find food and live in the park. Yet the park was established to preserve a unique concentration of plants and animals.

Painters of the Caves (1998) tells of art produced in Europe during the late Stone Age and is obviously not a science book per se. Here I started outside the box and then reached back in to explain how archaeologists and other scientists have pieced together the story of who the painters were, where they came from, how they lived and worked, when they lived, what they painted, and why they may have painted. The art content, I think, is enhanced by the underlying science, which introduces these remarkable early modern humans.

Flood: Wrestling with the Mississippi (1996a) unites history, geography, engineering, and ecology to tell the story of a mighty river that acts as if it had a will of its own. It is a river that "likes" to change its course, including its route to the Gulf of Mexico. Yet today some seven million people live and work along the Mississippi, and their livelihood is somehow linked to the river—to the rich soil of its floodplains, to the refineries and chemical plants that use its water, to businesses that supply farms and industries. The Mississippi and its tributaries form a major water highway in the heart of North America. Because it is vitally important to agriculture and industry, the Mississippi is held on course by tremendous works of engineering. Even so, a number of scientists think that it will one day break free—and that we should rethink our relationship with the river while there is still time.

These three books and the others I have written in recent years are all beautiful to look at, and this is probably the biggest change I've seen in nonfiction books for children over recent years. When I first wrote children's books, in the late 1950s, publishers tended to spend their production money chiefly on picture books for the very young. Nonfiction often had a low priority, and science books in particular (never the editors' favorites) were, to put the matter as kindly as possible, drab. Illustrations tended to be black-and-white line drawings, kept simple because they had to be reproduced on cheap paper stock. If I was lucky, a book might have an insert of glossy stock on which photographs would be reproduced.

Change has come about in part because of the almost universal use of offset printing, which has altered the economics of printing well-illustrated books. Television has inadvertently contributed mightily to the improvement. Never having known a world without color television or film, children today expect color in books. Publishers are providing it. They too have moved beyond the confines of the box.

I am pleased, of course, because I love the way my books look today. I'm also pleased because the change frees me to call for a variety of illustrations and a generous number of them. Illustrations are no longer something I think up after I've written the text and use chiefly to break up pages of type. Today I plan and write a book with illustrations in mind, using them to complement and extend the text—to help explain difficult concepts, to emphasize a point, and to include material that, while germane, does not really fit in the text proper. And sometimes a picture is indeed worth a thousand words:

even someone in love with the printed word (me) can see that it is much better to let the cave art speak for itself than to describe it.

It has to be said that I also love books—the way they look on my shelves, the way a book feels in my hands, the delicious sense of anticipation a new book stirs in me. And that is another reason why I'm happy that publishers have broken out of the box with children's nonfiction. The more attractive print books are, the more likely they are to survive in an electronic age.

References   Lauber, P. (1996a). *Flood: Wrestling with the Mississippi.* Washington, DC: National Geographic Society.

Lauber, P. (1996b). *Hurricanes: Earth's mightiest storms.* New York: Scholastic Press.

Lauber, P. (1998). *Painters of the caves.* Washington, DC: National Geographic Society.

Writing in the '90s

Rhoda Blumberg

There has been talk about books becoming ancient archives—that they are being replaced by movies, television, computer games, e-mail, and Internet chat rooms. To feed their need for entertainment, children while away their time in front of screens. An online program called *Great Books for Dummies* offers synopses and term papers so that young customers need not waste hours reading books assigned in school. Just a click of the mouse and a printout does the job of getting homework out of the way. Comic books offer another quick fix. *The Odyssey* (Homer, 1969), *The Adventures of Huckleberry Finn* (Twain, 1885), and *The Legend of Sleepy Hollow* (Irving, 1899) are among the many classic works "made easy" through cartoon treatment. If an assignment to read Victor Hugo's *The Hunchback of Notre Dame* (1834) seems too time-consuming, there are always other choices: a comic book version or a Disney full-color movie production.

Many young people take full advantage of computers to do quality research and to learn about literature. They are led to good books by their mouses and monitors. But there are too many others who know ways of avoiding serious reading. They do not realize they are depriving themselves of the enchantments derived from meaningful books. I must lure children with lucid writing that is not only thought provoking but also diverting and entertaining.

As a result of the new technology, my writing habits have changed drastically during the last decade. I still have library books stacked high in my workroom. Most of these have been obtained through interlibrary loan, after I have completed a computer search for a good bibliography and located the libraries that hold the books. I also have innumerable computer printouts of articles related to my writing. The computer enables me to retrieve archival documents located in libraries throughout the world. My recent bibliographies include sources found by means of the Internet.

I must be wary of essays entered on the Internet that are not reliable. As a result of new computer superhighways, more material is available than can be used. And some of this sea of information is mixed with misinformation. Anyone can enter an essay on any subject. I have learned to be careful about sources and depend on reputable scholars for trustworthy information. I still need libraries and seek the help of librarians.

I also tell my stories through illustrations. Once again, I resort to the newest technology by searching libraries and museums on the Internet, then sending e-mails and faxes to their photo duplication departments. Reproductions of paintings not only provide visual information, but also expose me, and my readers, to quality art. George Catlin, Alfred Jacob Miller, and Paul Kane depicted western landscapes and the many native tribes as Lewis and Clark saw them. Superb artists who accompanied Captain Cook on his explorations drew people, places, portraits, and landscapes, as well as detailed reproductions of native rites and customs. Scrolls, woodblock prints, and other delightful works of Japanese artists were incorporated into *Commodore Perry in the Land of the Shogun* (1985) and in my most recent book, *Shipwrecked: The True Adventures of a Japanese Boy* (2001). Cartoons, sketches, prints, and newspaper ads of the time entertain as well as illuminate the nineteenth-century gold rush era and the building of the first transcontinental railroad. As a result of my picture research, my life has been enriched by exposure to art that was new to me. The illustrations can also serve as a reader's gateway to art appreciation.

History is my passion. It is replete with true stories that are as dramatic as any tale ever imagined in fiction. Heroes, heroines, and ordinary people of the past are especially fascinating because they truly existed, and good nonfiction can make the past as real as the present. Good narrative history should be entertaining as well as informative.

Being in love with my subject inspires me to write with un-bounded enthusiasm. Well-chosen words create images and convey ideas that thrill me first, then impel me to share them with an audience of readers. I must be enthralled and captivated by people and events of the past before feeling qualified to describe them to others. My need to research and write has intensified throughout the years.

I sometimes envy novelists because, unlike nonfiction writers, they don't have to scrutinize evidence and show proof that their writings come from reliable sources. The stories I tell have to be based on solid documentation. Every fact must be checked for accuracy. I cannot invent anything, not even the weather, the size of a person's nose, or a horse of a different color. I am also at a disadvantage because I do not allow myself to invent dialogue, and I can't supply surprise endings. The finale is fixed in time and backed by facts.

But I am not disabled as a writer because I don't dream up plots. People and events from history are as engrossing and dramatic as anything in fiction. Stories from the past are especially fascinating because they truly took place. They deal with events that actually occurred and describe people who really existed.

Research is my addiction. I love playing detective in libraries, seeking topics, discovering stories, finding anecdotes, and ferreting out facts that not only add to knowledge, but also are often entertaining and amusing. Like Sherlock Holmes, I need a spyglass—in my case, to read small print. I also get to snoop by reading private diaries and letters without being accused of violating privacy.

Secondary sources, books written by historians, supply basic background information. Primary sources enthrall me. They bring me closer to the past and enable me to uncover stories I have not read in other books. I participate in events of long ago. In *Full Steam Ahead: The Race to Build a Transcontinental Railroad* (1996), I joined an excursion that had been described for me by recollections of a participant. I dined and danced on a riverboat, camped in the prairies, watched American Indians dance, and saw workers laying track. For *The Great American Gold Rush* (1989), I read an 1848 guide for gold prospectors that hoodwinked gullible readers into believing that chunks of pure gold, as large and as thick as both my hands outspread, lay on the surface of California's ground. Lieutenant Preble's *The Opening of Japan: A Diary of Discovery in the Far East, 1853–1856* (1962) introduced me to samurai, geishas, and sumo wrestlers who became bit players in *Commodore Perry in the Land of the Shogun*. I learned about life on a New England whaler for my most recent book, *Shipwrecked: The True Adventures of a Castaway Japanese Boy* (2001).

Writing in the 1990s meant using vocabularies guaranteed not to offend any individual. There are African Americans, not Negroes; Native Americans, not Indians; Inuits, not Eskimos; Asians, not Orientals; explorers, not discoverers. (Columbus didn't "discover" America; he encountered lands new to Europeans.) *Primitive* is another term that is viewed today as pejorative when referring to aborigines. And today's writers avoid describing any tribe as "uncivilized" just because its culture differs from that of mainstream United States. These word changes date one's writing, but it's also true that these changes keep changing (e.g., I understand that "Indian" for American Indian is now as acceptable as Native American).

I am especially pleased that today's history books include information about the roles that women and minorities played in the past. I love social history. Learning about customs, costumes, attitudes, and ideas of ordinary citizens allows us to identify with them. Although political history is usually the backbone of books about history, I like to flesh out the pages with reports, reactions, and stories about ordinary people who lived long ago.

Research material becomes more and more accessible through the computer, but interpreting and extracting relevant information and then writing a manuscript still require the thoughts and emotions of human beings. The groundwork can be prepared efficiently by a machine, but the creation of good books still needs the ideas, feelings, and abilities of disciplined authors. Through teachers and librarians, young people can be exposed to the supreme enchantment of reading quality books.

References

Blumberg, R. (1985). *Commodore Perry in the land of the shogun.* New York: Lothrop, Lee & Shepard.

Blumberg, R. (1989). *The great American gold rush.* New York: Bradbury Press.

Blumberg, R. (1996). *Full steam ahead: The race to build a transcontinental railroad.* Washington, DC: National Geographic Society.

Blumberg, R. (2001). *Shipwrecked! The true adventures of a Japanese Boy.* New York: HarperCollins.

Homer. (1969). *The odyssey.* Trans. Robert Fitzgerald. Garden City, NY: Doubleday, Anchor Books.

Hugo, V. (1834). *The hunchback of Notre-Dame.* Philadelphia: Carey, Lea and Blanchard.

Irving, W. (1899). *The legend of Sleepy Hollow.* New York: G. P. Putnam's Sons.

Preble, G. H. (1962). *The opening of Japan: A diary of discovery in the Far East, 1853–1856.* Ed. Boleslaw Szczesniak. Norman: University of Oklahoma Press.

Twain, M. (1885). *The adventures of Huckleberry Finn.* New York: Charles L. Webster.

Orbis Pictus Award Winners, 1990–2000

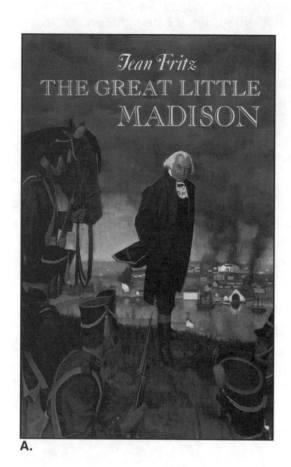

A.

B.

A. 1990: *The Great Little Madison* by Jean Fritz. **B. 1991:** *Franklin Delano Roosevelt* by Russell Freedman.

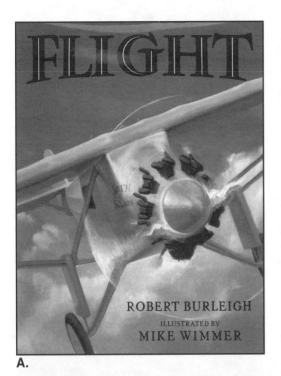

A.

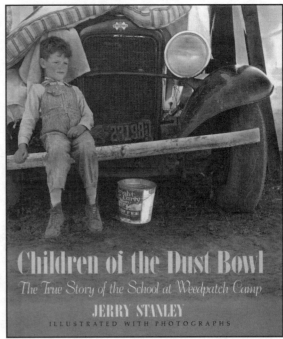

B.

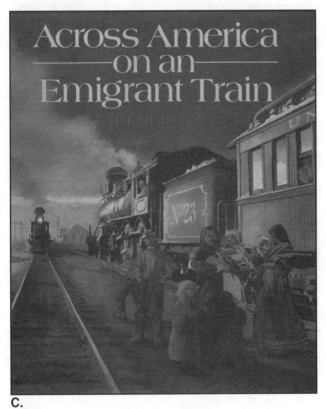

C.

A. 1992: *Flight: The Journey of Charles Lindbergh* by Robert Burleigh; illustrated by Mike Wimmer. **B. 1993:** *Children of the Dust Bowl: The True Story of the School at Weedpatch Camp* by Jerry Stanley. **C. 1994:** *Across America on an Emigrant Train* by Jim Murphy.

A.

B.

C.

A. 1995: *Safari beneath the Sea: The Wonder World of the North Pacific Coast* by Diane Swanson; photographs by the Royal British Columbia Museum. **B. 1996:** *The Great Fire* by Jim Murphy. **C. 1997:** *Leonardo da Vinci* by Diane Stanley.

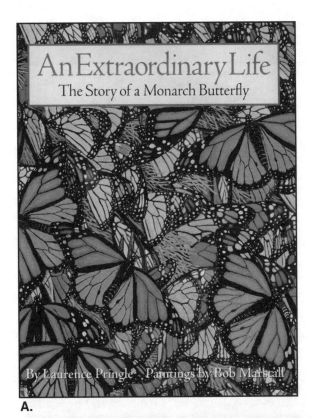

A.

B.

C.

A. 1998: *An Extraordinary Life: The Story of a Monarch Butterfly* by Laurence Pringle; paintings by Bob Marstall.
B. 1999: *Shipwreck at the Bottom of the World: The Extraordinary True Story of Shackleton and the* Endurance by Jennifer Armstrong. **C. 2000:** *Through My Eyes* by Ruby Bridges.

A World of Difference

Jennifer Owings Dewey

For fox or man the better plan
*   With unknown danger near,*
Is to go home and no more roam
*   Until the way be clear.*

Thornton Burgess,
The Adventures of Old Man Coyote

I remember being read to by a young Irish girl my parents hired as a nanny, though the year was 1943 and World War II caused a drop in the availability of "help." I no longer remember her name, only her voice, and the sweet, fresh smell of her. She used plain soap, I know now, nothing perfumed.

Sitting in her lap with eyes half-closed, I listened to her read and traveled to the places she described. I was the main character—hero or heroine, it didn't matter. I was Peter Rabbit, Mrs. Quack, or Jerry Muskrat swimming in the Smiling Pool.

The Irish girl was replaced by an English girl, and then, surprisingly, because we were at war with the Japanese, a skinny man whose name was Fuji. My father wanted to show he held no prejudices, so he hired a U.S.-born cook-nanny of Japanese extraction in the midst of the war with Japan. Fuji read aloud in a voice with a strong midwestern accent.

During Fuji's tenure, I began to hunger for reality in stories. Fuji indulged me, selecting nonfiction books to read aloud whenever possible. There were so few nonfiction titles for children in those days that Fuji often read the same book again and again.

Fuji was fired for two reasons. One was his habit of putting banana flavoring into everything he cooked. Second, he gave each of us four children, including my baby brother, nickels, pennies, and dimes. My father was firm about "gifts" given to his children. He sent Fuji packing.

This event caused me to question my father's motives in hiring Fuji in the first place. The cook-nanny's departure inspired a search in the family library for books about Japan. My investigation of what I then called "real books" required standing on various pieces of furniture placed so I could reach the highest shelves. One afternoon the inevitable happened. I crashed to the floor, knocking chairs, lamps, and tables every which way, sending volumes flying around the room. The commotion was enough to summon a furious nanny-of-the-week, a woman with blue hair and blazing pink eyes.

Mrs. Jamison scolded me, saying, "You have no business in your parents' library."

Instead of deterring me, her words set the stage for even more raids on the library shelves for adult nonfiction titles. I became addicted to stories of daring mountain climbers, Arctic and Antarctic exploration, perilous journeys across vast wildernesses, the Greeks, the Romans, and kings and queens of England, France, and Spain.

My curiosity about Japan and the Japanese people was left unsatisfied. The library contained nothing to read on the subject. There was even more to be frustrated about—I craved true stories about wild animals, and I could find none.

In 1946, Sally Carrighar's book *One Day on Beetle Rock* was published. My grandfather, knowing of my eagerness for books about animals, sent me the slim volume for my birthday. Reading it changed my life, for within its covers I found all I had been wanting in the way of clear, vivid, wonderfully precise words about the lives of animals.

Not only did Carrighar write beautifully, but she also elevated a bear, a weasel, and a deer mouse (among others) to the level of heroes and heroines. Her descriptions of these creatures gave authority to nature writing. She wrote without imposing human characteristics on the animals. Her awareness of how the mule deer's lips moved when browsing twig ends illuminated the simplest events in the wild world, invisible to my eyes until her books appeared.

Through reading *One Day at Beetle Rock, One Day at Teton Marsh* (1947), *Icebound Summer* (1953), and Carrighar's other books, I came to trust and believe in natural history writing as a valid genre. This conviction has grown with time.

Great surges of change have occurred since I was young in attitudes toward writing about the natural world. Writing nonfiction natural history is now recognized as important, on a par with writing history, biography, and political tomes. A long list can be drawn up of accomplished writers devoted to writing natural history, when once the list was short.

When I began writing nonfiction for children, I wanted my books to describe, as Sally Carrighar's did, the lives of animals without the imposition of human activity in order to create a true sense of what it is to be a coyote, a rattlesnake, or a garden spider. The beauty of this approach was its honesty. To focus on a day in the life of a kangaroo rat would, I believed, bring to the child reader an

awareness of this small furry rodent that would inspire an understanding of nature well beyond the rat's activities. The wild world
deserved to be described without compromise.

Eventually I began to yearn for a way to describe the boundary between the wild world and the human one. I saw that without
any mention of human activity in stories about animals there was a
missing piece. That piece was the link between ourselves and *them*.
My book *Wildlife Rescue* (1994) was my first effort to bring together
events in the lives of wild animals and the human response to those
events. While doing the research for this book, I was moved when I
discovered the shared responsibility many people feel, those who
help to rehabilitate wild animals hit by cars, mistakenly (or deliberately) shot by hunters, or electrocuted by high-tension wires.

The book was a turning point. I have become increasingly
interested in personalizing nonfiction so that child readers find the
science aspects more accessible. In my rattlesnake book, for example,
I used no fictional devices but described personal experiences with
rattlesnakes to make the narrative alive and engaging.

At the beginning of the twenty-first century, the necessity of
emphasizing our dependence on planet Earth and its nonhuman
residents becomes more crucial than ever. The changes in my thinking about nonfiction have been motivated by a desire to be a spokes-
person for the environment, wildness, and wilderness. In addition,
the writing life brings with it a deeply personal evolution of self, one
that is never still.

Writing as a way of life means anticipating constant change.
The passage of time has brought greater demands on authors to
create books popular enough that children will read them again and
again despite almost limitless distractions, from video games to the
Internet. I have remained stubbornly attached to my ideas about
clarity, honesty, and presenting what is true without bias, while
remaining aware of the dangers of adhering to these principles.

One primary fear is that of not getting published. Worse yet
would be giving in to the negative forces at work that erode original
intentions. Signals are everywhere, urging authors to conform, to
write marketable books without substance. An author who does not
remain absolutely positive about what he or she believes in and
wishes to do will get washed away.

Since starting as a writer, I have seen my books given as much
attention—in design and quality of paper, print, and binding—as
fine fiction titles. There is no obvious discrimination against them, as
there once was when nonfiction was "stepsister" to fiction. And yet
the marketing of nonfiction remains less understood than that of
fiction. Nonfiction claims a smaller audience of readers and probably
always will, but it is an audience fully devoted, avid, and loyal.

I recognize and appreciate high standards and expectations set by those making publishing decisions. Every new idea is a challenge, not only to achieve for my own sake, but also for the sake of those who will read what I write. Reviewers can be tough, especially on nonfiction, in which factual information must be correct and clearly stated. I often choose subjects that are not mainstream. I have been called "an advocate for bats, spiders, and snakes, animals with too few legs, or too many." I like this distinction. I feel as I did as a child, that "lowly" creatures, as well as the more "evolved," deserve to be recognized and understood if any of us are to survive. I am glad for the heightened awareness over the environment and greater attention given to the natural sciences. The minds and hearts of children are enlightened, not prejudiced, depending on the quality of nonfiction books available to them, as well as the fiction they read.

There is a world of difference between the stories I loved when I was small, those about Hooty the Owl, Reddy Fox, Jimmy Skunk, and Old Man Coyote, and what nonfiction authors write today. Society has changed, grown up, matured. I know most of the readers of my books experience a deep connection to nature, giving me a greater responsibility to contribute worthy manuscripts.

As a writer, I enjoy the dialogue between editor and author, even though this may include giving up on an idea not compelling enough to make it in today's unforgiving marketplace. The dialogue can be heartbreaking when a subject fascinating to me is considered too nontraditional to be published. Our world is more complex than ever and young audiences harder to reach, reading often turning up last on a list of favorite pastimes. Still, in the last ten years the potential for publishing nonfiction of high quality has grown and expanded.

Once some years ago, standing on an ice floe in Antarctica out of sight of the ship that had brought us there, I and two companions stood looking into the white distance, a wilderness as profound as any left on Earth. None of us spoke. We were awed, without being frightened, made to feel small, without being reduced. I feel this about my work as a writer. Time passes, my fortunes rise and fall, I am a small part of a much bigger scene, and yet I am excited, always, by what is to come, what there is next to explore, work on, write.

References   Burgess, Thornton W. (1916). *The Adventures of Old Man Coyote*. Boston: Little, Brown.

Carrighar, S. (1944). *One day on Beetle Rock*. New York: Knopf.

Carrighar, S. (1947). *One day at Teton Marsh*. New York: Knopf.

Carrighar, S. (1953). *Icebound summer*. New York: Knopf.

Dewey, J. O. (1994). *Wildlife rescue: The work of Dr. Kathleen Ramsay*. Honesdale, PA: Boyds Mills Press.

12 One World, Many Religions

Mary Pope Osborne

In the early 1990s, Knopf Books for Young Readers asked me to write a children's book that presented an overview of the major religions of the world. It was a thrilling idea. I'd always been fascinated by the different faiths. I had a degree in religion from the University of North Carolina and had spent time after graduating traveling through Islamic and Hindu countries. Nevertheless, I balked at the proposal. I was not an authority on the world religions. It seemed audacious for me to assume I could corral such complicated, potentially controversial material and present it to children.

My interest in the subject and my concern about the need for such a book, however, soon triumphed over my fears of inadequacy. While visiting schools in connection with my other books, I became aware that unlike the schools of my own childhood, many today enroll children from many different religious backgrounds. I also became aware that very few books about the different faiths of the world were available in school libraries. I was amazed to learn that some teachers thought it was unconstitutional to have such books in schools. I explained that only books that try to indoctrinate or convert the reader to a particular faith are considered out-of-bounds. Books with objective information are allowed. But for the most part, those sorts of books were not only unavailable in school libraries—they simply did not exist at all.

I finally took a deep breath and decided to write *One World, Many Religions* (1996) in an attempt to fill this need. I knew I would have to approach the task not with the knowledge of an expert, but with the passion of an *enthusiast*. Would this passion be enough, though, to drive me to acquire the knowledge I would need to acquaint children with the history and practices of Christianity, Judaism, Islam, Hinduism, Buddhism, Confucianism, and Taoism? Would it be enough to help me sort through mountains of information and distill the essential elements in a way that was clear, respectful, and objective?

Over the next three years, I often had my doubts. The more I read about each faith, the more complicated the subject became. Many of the sources I consulted were biased and dated. Sometimes books on the same subject offered conflicting interpretations of religious philosophy. Many were written in such a complex way that it was impossible to cull the basic facts.

The very profusion and confusion of information, though, began to fuel my fervor. I felt an overwhelming urge to create order out of the chaos—not unlike the urgency one feels untangling coils of holiday lights. The reward promised to be similar: single, individual strands of small glowing lights circling one world.

For me, the key to order and clarity became *story*. I realized that the basis of almost all the major faiths was a central story, a *sacred story*, from which its most important rituals and practices were derived. The role of storyteller was a comfortable role for me. Of the more than twenty books I had published up to that point, only three had been nonfiction: biographies of George Washington, Benjamin Franklin, and Christopher Columbus. All the others had been novels, storybooks, or the retellings of mythology and legends.

I happily approached the beginning of each section of the book with the heart and mind of a storyteller. After I told the sacred story of a particular religion, I branched out into factual information: a brief history of the faith, then an overview of its fundamental practices and rituals. I decided that children primarily needed to know the most common, day-to-day forms of worship in cultures, the glue that holds families and communities together. So I chose to convey that basic information in as concise a way as possible, without getting into complicated philosophy or dogma, or information about divisions and sects within a faith.

I was fortunate to have good editorial and scholarly advice to help clarify and verify my text. Three different editors worked on the book in the course of its evolution. Each chapter was sent for review to an expert on the particular faith.

I also consulted "ordinary people." Having the advantage of living in multicultural New York City, I talked to Islamic cab drivers, Indian restaurateurs, and Buddhist grocery store owners. Everyone I queried seemed pleased and eager to help. They graciously gave specific and careful answers to my questions, helping me to better understand the priorities and perspective of their faith.

From the beginning, I felt it was important that the visual design of the book work with the text to help clarify the information. My editors and I had agreed that the book was to be illustrated with photographs rather than with drawings and paintings. I believed that presenting the photographs in an old-fashioned linear, narrative style—rather than a collage style, such as that in an Eyewitness series book—would enhance the particular order I was after. As I wrote each chapter, I designated where photographs should go and what sort of images we should try to get. I also decided that the book needed a time line, a world map showing the different faiths, and a glossary of religious terms.

Fortunately, the publisher's art department was receptive to most of my ideas. Over the three years of working on the book, our method of collaboration became routine: I listed the kinds of photographs I felt necessary to amplify the text; the lists were given to a gifted photo researcher who gathered a number of possible slides; and then the photo researcher, the art director, editor, and I met regularly to review the photos and choose our favorites. We found we were invariably most excited about the photographs of young people participating in acts of worship, such as an Afgani boy reading the Koran, a Hindu girl celebrating the Festival of Lights, or two young girls joyfully singing a hymn in a Harlem church.

When I first began writing *One World, Many Religions*, I had feared that it would be difficult to write from a completely objective point of view while still creating a book that conveyed the awesome power of each religion. This eventually proved less difficult than I had anticipated. Even today, when I look for the hundredth time at the faces of the children in these photographs, I find it impossible not to be moved by the wonder and mystery of their faiths. I know these children evoke in young readers respect and honor for their cultures and ways of worship. These children, in the end, were the small lights that glow.

Reference   Osborne, M. P. (1996). *One world, many religions: The ways we worship*. New York: Knopf.

Nonfiction, 1999

Jean Fritz

Thirty years ago when I started writing nonfiction for children, I was warned that I might find a hostile audience, if I found an audience at all. At that time, children were apt to be suspicious of nonfiction as another ploy adults used to lure them to the academic world. I would have to invent dialogue, I was told, in order to disguise the factual nature of my books. And when I examined juvenile biographies, I saw that this advice was being followed by other writers. Indeed, I could almost predict the points when an eighteenth-century hero or heroine would have to break into pseudo-twentieth-century speech—yes, complete with unearned quotation marks.

Of course, it is easy to see how some writers with their eye on the school market might be seduced into such formulaic writing. I am constantly receiving letters begging for tips on how to write a successful biography. These people seem to take for granted that writing nonfiction is a quick study, a seat taken on the outside of their story. This is not so. Nonfiction, like fiction, has to be written from the inside out. Only after total immersion does the material begin to take shape. Only after you feel completely at home with the background and circumstances of a life, only after you understand how and why your subject became what he or she became—only then can you sense what your story might turn out to be.

I have never been tempted in nonfiction either to preach or teach, yet I have never emerged from the experience without learning something about life itself. Actually, I have only been trying to fill in the blank spaces between the lines of my old childhood textbooks, fill them with real people and true stories. If I use an informal, conversational style, it is because I want to share my discoveries, not lecture on them. So when I find my biographies shelved under "fiction," I get upset. The explanation always is, "But your books seem like fiction. They're fun to read and might get lost on the nonfiction shelves." But nonfiction has changed dramatically since I began writing. Today, with all the new, talented writers contributing such diverse material to those nonfiction shelves, children surely will discover that books can be fun no matter which shelf they live on.

For me, the fun of writing nonfiction has always been in the research. I read as if I were writing a doctoral dissertation, discarding as well as collecting as I go. But the best part comes after the reading when I make my onsite visits, usually to the home of my character or at least to some place closely connected to him or her, where my book knowledge is translated into something that feels like memory. I treasure these personal visits when the people I know so much about suddenly spring to life. I think of the time I stood on the Madisons' back porch, looking over their lovely plantation and imagining the path James and Dolly took on their walks together. I think of going to Boston in search of John Hancock. His house is no longer standing; in its place is the State House, which was in some disarray when I was there because the foundation was being strengthened. When I asked about the bricks that had been dug up and were strewn on the ground, I was told they had been authenticated. They were eighteenth-century bricks made in England and had been, if not in Hancock's house, certainly in one of his outbuildings. That night when I flew back to New York I had one of those bricks, wrapped in newspaper, in my bag. It sits in front of my fireplace now, an intimate and abiding expression of the warmth I feel for that cocky show-off who "wanted everyone to like him."

And I think of the visit my husband and I made to Sam Houston's last home, where his bedroom, they claim, is just as he left it. How could I help but notice the pair of American Indian moccasins beside his bed? They were so small, and yet I knew that Sam had been a big man, over six feet tall. "We think they must have been his teenage moccasins," the curator explained. It was hard to believe. A seventy-year-old man hanging on to his teenage moccasins! But the next day, looking through the archives at the state capitol, I came across the information that Sam Houston had unusually small feet. I felt as if Sam were talking to me. Yes, those were his moccasins after all—likely the last thing he'd slipped his bare feet into!

I often wondered if I would ever be satisfied with a biography that didn't include this kind of substitute for a face-to-face meeting. Then, five years ago I went to the hospital for what was supposed to be a minor operation on my back. I haven't walked unaided since. Something went wrong on the operating table, and I've had to get along using either a wheelchair or a walker, which means that I am not as independent as I once was. At about the same time, my husband died. Since he had shared my little research excursions, I asked myself if I would write again, if I even wanted to.

Although this essay is supposed to be about the general field of nonfiction, it is hard for me to keep my personal experience out of it. I decided to stay in our old house, living alone, and I also decided not to look too far ahead. I would act as if I were continuing to write, and see what happened. I was working on a biography of Lafayette at the time, and I knew that if the circumstances had been different, I would have gone to France. Instead, I attended a teachers convention and met a teacher from Fayetteville, North Carolina—the first town in the United States to be named for Lafayette. The people of this town give an annual party for Lafayette on his birthday, September 6. This teacher invited me to attend. And I did. When the guests stood to toast Lafayette and sing "The Marseilles," I knew I need not worry about not going to France. If Lafayette had known about this celebration, he would have been here. And so, I felt, he was.

I started working on the Lost Colony next, and again I was lucky. When I accidentally heard about a dig being undertaken on Cape Hatteras for Lost Colony clues, I longed to be a part of it, even if I couldn't dig. An anthropologist friend agreed to go with me. I took a plane to Norfolk where she met me, and we proceeded to the site. Nothing was found that day, but the day before a ring had been uncovered with the crest of a rampant lion on it. Consultation with the Department of Heraldry in England uncovered the information that the ring had been the property of the Kendall family, two of whom had been associated with that time and place. When I held that ring in the palm of my hand, I felt the full weight of its history. I came back from that dig rejuvenated. Yes, I could go on. One way or another, I could.

Work on the Lost Colony has been put aside for the moment, for a few weeks ago lightning struck. A friend and I went to Beacon, New York, where a twenty-four-feet-high bronze horse was being exhibited prior to being shipped to Milan as a gift from the American people to the Italians. A Renaissance enthusiast from Pennsylvania wanted the gift of this horse to be a gesture of appreciation to Leonardo da Vinci, who had made a similar horse five hundred years before that had been decimated by an invading French army. The Beacon horse took my breath away. It looked like a mythological horse about to take off, probably for the sky. On the spur of the moment, I approached the young man in charge of the project and told him that I'd like to do a picture book for children about the horse. The long and short of it was that the "horse" people agreed; my publisher agreed; and I have just returned from Milan, accompanied by my daughter, where the horse was celebrated and unveiled.

I really can't say much about the general field of nonfiction. I'm too excited about the fact that I am still in it.

Serendipity, Detective Work, and Worry: One Nonfiction Writer's Journey through the '90s

Jim Murphy

Like most writers of nonfiction, I work on projects long before they appear as finished books. That's why my 1990s nonfiction actually began back in 1984 when I started collecting material for my first book about the Civil War, *The Boys' War* (1990).

That was the year I encountered a memoir written by Elisha Stockwell Jr. that detailed his nearly four years of service in the Union Army. Now remember, this was well before Ken Burns and his PBS documentary reawakened popular interest in this conflict and the plight of the common soldier. My studies of the Civil War had been limited to school courses using standard reference texts featuring politicians, generals, and long, overly complicated discussions of troop movements and military tactics. The soldiers who actually fought the war weren't discussed in much detail; mention of boys was limited to saying they were drummers in military bands. When I learned that Elisha was just fifteen when he signed enlistment papers to fight, I remember thinking, "I didn't know kids did that!"

I wondered if the fact that kids took an active part in such an important event in our history—as opposed to merely having it happen all around them—would pull young readers into a book on the subject. The "I didn't know that!" factor also energized me, made me want to know more about the hidden parts of the Civil War and the role played by very young soldiers.

The initial challenge was to find more boys like Elisha, a search made more difficult because no military reports or histories devoted solely to them existed. Fortunately, I love doing research, which I see as a form of detective work minus the trench coat and gun. I spent the next few years very happily poking through the files of historical societies, searching battalion histories, and hunting the shelves of libraries and antiquarian bookstores. The result was several notebooks filled with the names of boy soldiers and information about them.

Along with scores of names came something else: quotes. These boys, and Civil War soldiers in general, were remarkably literate and seemed to love writing down what was happening to them and what they felt. No topic, it seemed, was too small for their attention. They wrote about sneaking off to enlist, training and dealing with older soldiers, army food (or more frequently, the complete lack of it), and the fighting. One boy even described how four soldiers sleeping cheek to jowl in a tiny tent could execute a turn in their sleep to military commands—"To the left. Turn!" Most important, they spoke about their constant fear and loneliness.

To this point in my nonfiction writing, I had used quotes sparingly, a brief one here, another there, with me writing most of the text. But reading hundreds of these boys' letters, diaries, and journals made it clear that they could speak far more eloquently about their experiences and emotions than I could ever hope to. So I decided to use their quotes—their voices—as much as possible to let them talk about the war.

One aspect of the project gave me pause. I wasn't sure how graphic I should be when it came to discussing the gore of battle. This was the mid-1980s and feelings about the Vietnam War and the antiwar protest movement were still somewhat raw. People seemed to consciously avoid discussion of that era, probably so they wouldn't offend or upset anyone who didn't feel the same as they did. At what point, I wondered, would descriptions of the gruesome scenes turn off readers?

Happily, these young Civil War soldiers came to my rescue. Their descriptions of the mayhem of fighting and of the dead and wounded were direct and honest, but never gratuitous. In fact, these very clear descriptions led me to another decision about the book— that I would use as many photographs as possible to illustrate it. Photos, especially of the dead, have a power and impact lacking in line drawings, which tend to play down and romanticize the carnage of battle.

I came away from *The Boys' War* with a real determination to do another book showing young people actively participating in our history, and to use their voices to propel the narrative along. How that book came about is a roundabout story, so bear with me.

For a long time I had wanted to do a book about Abraham Lincoln, and I'd been gathering details about his life and trying to come up with some sort of approach to the project. Obviously, one big obstacle stood in the way—Russell Freedman's wonderful and award-winning *Lincoln: A Photobiography* (1987). With Russell's book already established as a classic, any new book about Lincoln would have to be truly unique and distinguished to survive. And quite frankly, nothing I cooked up came close to this criterion.

I was, however, still fascinated by Lincoln, especially with the way he asked, then demanded, that his army commanders meet the enemy in a head-to-head battle. The war had dragged along for three years and casualties were mounting at an alarming rate—and with them, pressure from critics to negotiate a settlement to the dispute. Lincoln knew that any such settlement would probably mean the acceptance of states' rights and, with it, the institution of slavery. That was clearly unacceptable to him; but he needed a victory in order to hold the North together politically and thus be able to pursue the war to a satisfactory conclusion. His wish for such a confrontation was answered at Gettysburg.

Of course, as interesting as I found this side of Lincoln, I knew perfectly well that in and of itself it probably wouldn't grab hold of many young readers. Among other things, it wasn't active or immediate. After all, how many times could I show Lincoln hovering over incoming messages from generals at the front and snapping out impatient replies? So I started going through all of my previous Civil War research, hoping something in it might inspire a different way to shape the material.

It was while reading through my notebooks from *The Boys' War* that I noticed something odd. Two young soldiers, one a Southern lieutenant named John Dooley, the other a Northern corporal named Thomas Galway, talked about a clump of trees in very similar terms. Where, I wondered, were they during the fighting? I got out a map of the battlefield to trace their movements during the three-day battle and realized that they may have come within one hundred feet of each other during Pickett's Charge on July 3. Now here was a coincidence I couldn't ignore!

Both young men kept journals throughout their army careers, so I had my central characters and voices. When I reread their accounts, I discovered I had much more than this. Both documented in marvelous detail their lives from the moment they began marching toward Gettysburg four weeks before the battle until well after the final shot was fired. Dooley was badly wounded at Gettysburg and spent the rest of the war in a prison hospital; Galway was slightly injured but was able to help pick up the wounded before marching off to the next battle.

What if my book traced their journeys to Gettysburg from start to finish, I wondered. Readers would watch two great armies moving closer and closer to a terrible confrontation through the daily experiences of these boys. Was this enough of a story line to draw readers along? I hoped so.

Of course, the idea of having a story line in a book of nonfiction wasn't new; many adult nonfiction books are constructed and written in a way that reads like a novel, such as Irving Werstein's *The Blizzard of '88* (1960). But focusing on a line of action meant a number of other decisions about my project fell into place. For instance, Gettysburg is one of the most thoroughly documented battles of the Civil War, with literally tens of thousands of pages written about it. Yet I worried that any attempt to cover the three days of fighting in a comprehensive way would overwhelm and smother my main characters and their stories. I opted instead to cut the non-Dooley/Galway information to the bare essentials. Make sure readers understand what the Civil War and the battle are about, I told myself every day, but keep the text lean and moving forward.

Cutting details is sometimes a painful procedure. I often sit around mumbling things like, "Okay, okay, this fact isn't absolutely necessary, but it's so bizarre kids will love it." I was able to calm myself a little on this score by taking some of the information that didn't make it into the main text and using it in the illustration captions. This created problems for the designer—how do you keep the illustrations large enough to have impact and still work in three or four lines of text?—but I thought it added value to the captions that young readers would appreciate. I've continued doing the same in subsequent books.

The decision to focus on a story line had another consequence. I didn't want anyone—reviewers, librarians, or readers—to think I had made up anything when describing a scene or to enhance the drama or emotion. Since I knew I would have to include many everyday details, such as what the weather was like on a particular day at 6 A.M., I made a lot of research journeys in search of very specific tidbits. If I found the detail, fine; if I didn't, the text had to be changed. I spent a good deal of profitable time scanning Civil War photographs with my magnifying glass for incidental information.

What happened to Abraham Lincoln? His role as an active and demanding commander-in-chief is a part of the main text, of course, but I eventually chose to go into his address at the Gettysburg cemetery in much more detail. Why? After the crash and chaos of the battle, the 269-word Gettysburg Address provided a gracious and natural conclusion to both the battle and Dooley's and Galway's stories.

Several reviewers criticized *The Long Road to Gettysburg* (1992) for not being an exhaustive history of the battle, so I suppose my decision to cut out a great deal of background information did have a negative impact. My only response is that I never intended to write a definitive history; I wanted to write an experience book that would let readers see and feel what this battle was like.

When I finished work on this book, my editor at Clarion, the late Dorothy Briley, urged me—actually, she told me—not to do another Civil War book for a while. There had been a rush of Civil War books following the Ken Burns documentary and Dorothy, wisely, felt any additional ones might be lost in the crowd. So there I was, week after week, trying to figure out what subject to tackle next.

I do this by reading all sorts of books, fiction and nonfiction; by gazing at the ceiling of my office and thinking; by washing dishes or picking up debris left around the house by my two sons. One day I was looking through my postcard collection dealing with trains and train travel and enjoying a visual journey—on board the New York Central's Empire State Express; on The Western Flyer stopped at a Pennsylvania station; chugging along the Plains aboard the Rocky Mountain Limited. Somewhere along the line I found myself wondering if I might be able to put together a book about transcontinental train travel.

I enjoy playing with book ideas—figuring out what sort of information would be appropriate, how the chapters might be organized, what illustrations would complement and enhance the text. Research helps me clarify such thinking, though it usually means I reject an idea and move on to another. In this case, however, my readings about transcontinental train travel led to a pleasant discovery—namely, that in 1879 Robert Louis Stevenson had made a frantic trip from Scotland to California because he had learned that the woman he loved, Fanny Van de Grift Osbourne, was seriously ill. Stevenson was an impoverished young writer at the time, so he was forced to travel as cheaply as possible—in steerage aboard the ship and by emigrant class on the train. What is more, he later wrote two short but lively books about his experiences in and his feelings about the United States, *The Amateur Emigrant* (1895) and *Across the Plains with Other Memories and Essays* (1892). With Stevenson as the central character, I set about putting together what would become *Across America on an Emigrant Train* (1993).

Stevenson was twenty-nine years old at the time, so I wouldn't be able to write a "history made by kids" book. On the other hand, he was such a fabulous travel guide that I was confident his words and his story could entice readers to keep turning the pages. My narrative would stitch his story together while providing historical background on a number of related subjects, including the building of the transcontinental railroad, why so many trains crashed back then, the effect railroads had on Native Americans, and so on. And the fact that he had to travel so cheaply meant I could draw parallels between his experiences and those of our immigrant ancestors.

I realized one modestly interesting thing during the writing phase of this book. I found myself more and more annoyed with the way I was putting together sentences, worrying that they weren't lively enough, interesting enough—they weren't enough! Then I saw why. I had used a great many passages from Stevenson's two books, and my writing was simply pale and bloodless in comparison.

You have to understand something about me as a writer: I worry all the time about everything. Have I said enough about this person? Or too much? Have I included too much background information on the subject? Or not enough? Have I represented this group of individuals fairly? In part, worrying is the way I challenge myself to stay alert and focused, to do the best work I can before my editors get involved. Some of this worry is also a natural response to a fact of the market—there are a lot of extremely good nonfiction writers out there competing for review attention and sales. I assume I'm not alone in doing this and that most other writers go through a similar, if less painful, process to do a better job.

In this case, the challenge was to improve the quality of my writing by playing with sentences, moving phrases, and adding or deleting words, again and again. It goes without saying that the level of my writing never came close to matching Stevenson's. But I think the exercise pushed me in a positive way and may have resulted in a smoother-flowing text.

Even as *Across America on an Emigrant Train* went to the printer in 1993, I was going through a rough period with one of my other publishers, Scholastic. My editor there, Dianne Hess, and I had already done several picture books together, and they had, to my mind anyway, received good reviews and sold fairly well. Despite what seemed like a successful record, Dianne rejected one proposal of mine, then another. Naturally, I wanted to know what was wrong with these ideas, and she did her best to answer: the ideas were nice, she said, but didn't really grab her attention.

Hmmm. I tried again and was rejected again. What's the problem now? I asked. She wasn't sure the book would appeal to a wide enough reading audience. Another proposal was written and shot down. Why? I inquired. It didn't seem active or dramatic enough, she told me.

Our phone conversations and written correspondence about all of this were pleasant and businesslike. Dianne is an intelligent editor and a superb book person, so I trust that when she says something isn't right, it isn't right. But as rejection piled on rejection,

I began to wonder if I'd ever be able to put together an idea that she would want to publish. Yes, I worry about this, too.

Here's where serendipity, mixed with a touch of desperation, can come in handy. Around the time the latest rejection arrived, I was in a used bookstore in Vermont and came upon a copy of *Chicago and the Great Conflagration* (Colbert & Chamberlin, 1872). It had been published a month or so after the 1871 fire that destroyed one-quarter of Chicago and contained a number of firsthand recollections of the fire. Since I enjoy reading all sorts of firsthand accounts, I bought it.

Two weeks later I was thumbing through the book when I remembered something from my research days on *The Boys' War*. While rounding up the names of young soldiers, I had stumbled on fourteen-year-old Claire Innis's account of being lost in a panicking crowd and trying to outrun the flames that were eating up Chicago. A desperate hunt for those long-forgotten notes followed, but I'm happy to say that several days later I was able to read Claire's account once again.

Claire gave me a young person to include in a narrative, and her recollections were certainly active and dramatic. In addition to Claire, I also had a number of other people with interesting, exciting stories to tell.

The nice thing about the Chicago fire is that it has its own built-in story line. The fire starts small, it quickly leaps over the heads of the firefighters and spreads out of control, and then, just as it seems it will burn forever, it goes out when rain begins to fall a few days later. I had also noticed that most of the survivors, including newspaper reporters and insurance adjusters, referred to the fire as a living, sentient creature. That's why the fire is treated almost like another character in my book, though I cautioned myself to steer clear of out-and-out anthropomorphism.

These pieces of the book fell into place over the course of two or three months of research, which is fairly quick for me. But something still bothered me. The idea had several nice themes I could develop—the power of nature unleashed, the price of greed and vanity, and the physical and emotional resilience of humans, to name a few. But was this enough?

The Great Fire had been headline news across the country when it happened, but its importance in our nation's history has faded over time. Few history texts even bother to mention it these days, and I doubted that it was part of many school curriculums outside the state of Illinois. I worried that teachers and librarians around the country might find the subject matter too specialized or too local in nature to warrant inclusion in their collections. My job, then, was to pull out other themes that might broaden the book's appeal.

I didn't have a clue as to what they might be. Normally, I would have plunged ahead with research, hoping to unearth the answers along the way. This time I decided to approach the book in a slightly different way. I put off doing more research and instead spent a month or so writing the opening chapter. My reason was simple: I wanted to capture on paper the pacing and phrases that were banging around in my head before they faded away or, worse, before whatever energy they had evaporated. New information, details, and themes could be worked into this chapter at a later date.

While working on this chapter, I tried to puzzle out what those other themes might be. To help my thought process, I read several books by James Cross Giblin. Jim's books all have strong themes, and I learn a great deal by studying how he establishes and builds on them chapter by chapter to a satisfying payoff at the conclusion. This is especially true in *Walls: Defenses throughout History* (1984) and *Charles A. Lindbergh: A Human Hero* (1997).

When a rough draft of Chapter 1 was finished, I put it in a drawer and went on with the rest of the research with an eye open for a detail that might be built into a workable theme or themes. That detail came from Ross Miller's book, *American Apocalypse: The Great Fire and the Myth of Chicago* (1990). Buried in the notes at the back of his book is mention of a rally staged by German American citizens who were upset by the new building codes passed after the fire. It seems that these codes raised the cost of putting up a house to a point where many citizens couldn't afford to rebuild. Instead, they were forced to sell their land and move to cheaper, less regulated sections of town. As this happened, the price of land went up, so that other poor and middle-class residents whose houses hadn't been destroyed began selling off their property to take advantage of the hot real estate market.

Before the fire, it wasn't unusual for grand residences to be right around the corner from smaller, more humble ones. After the fire, the more well-to-do citizens were increasingly isolated from other economic classes of people. The gulf between various groups was more than physical, however.

Several official reports attempted to fix blame for the fire and the panic in the streets on the city's poorest citizens, and conveniently brushed aside several obvious government contributions to the fire, such as the miles of city streets and sidewalks made of wood. What surprised me most was how vile and personal these attacks could be. The O'Learys were routinely attacked as ignorant drunks and arsonists for profit; firemen (mostly Irish) were labeled cowardly and useless; the rioting was blamed on "blear-eyed, drunken, and diseased wretches, males and females, half naked, ghastly, with painted cheeks, cursing and uttering ribald jests as they drifted along" (White, 1871). The extreme nature of the language further distanced those with power from those without it. Suspicions and distrust grew between groups and eventually resulted in riots in the twentieth century. Although these tensions and the rioting would probably have happened without the fire, the fire speeded up the process.

When I finally had all of this in place, I wrote Dianne to ask if she would like me to burn down Chicago a second time—on paper, of course. To my relief, she said yes to *The Great Fire* (1995).

As you can tell, my nonfiction journey has been one of little steps—stumbling on interesting subjects and fresh voices, doing detective work, learning from other writers, listening to my editors, playing with ideas and words, worrying, and bringing out story lines and themes. Not everything I've tried has worked; not everything I try in the future will work either. The nice thing is to be around for another decade of chance finds, challenges, and worry. The journey has already begun!

References

Colbert, E., & Chamberlin, E. (1872). *Chicago and the great conflagration*. Cincinnati: C. F. Vent.

Freedman, R. (1987). *Lincoln: A photobiography*. New York: Clarion Books.

Giblin, J. C. (1984). *Walls: Defenses throughout history*. Boston: Little, Brown.

Giblin, J. C. (1997). *Charles A. Lindbergh: A human hero*. New York: Clarion Books.

Miller, R. (1990). *American apocalypse: The great fire and the myth of Chicago*. Chicago: University of Chicago Press.

Murphy, J. (1990). *The boys' war: Confederate and Union soldiers talk about the Civil War*. New York: Clarion Books.

Murphy, J. (1992). *The long road to Gettysburg*. New York: Clarion Books.

Murphy, J. (1993). *Across America on an emigrant train*. New York: Clarion Books.

Murphy, J. (1995). *The great fire*. New York: Scholastic.

Stevenson, R. L. (1892). *Across the Plains with other memories & essays*. New York: Charles Scribner's Sons.

Stevenson, R. L. (1895). *The amateur emigrant: From the Clyde to Sandy Hook*. Chicago: Stone and Kimball.

Werstein, I. (1960). *The blizzard of '88*. New York: Crowell.

White, H. (1871). Letter to M. Halstead, reprinted in the *Cincinnati Commercial*, October 1871.

III An Annotated Bibliography of Orbis Pictus Winners, Honor Books, and Recommended Titles, 1990–1999

Edited by Julie M. Jensen

Contributing reviewers include Elaine M. Aoki, Ruth Nathan, and Karen Patricia Smith

In the first decade of the Orbis Pictus Award, 187 titles were recognized as outstanding examples of nonfiction literature for children. Ten books won the award, 27 were designated as honor books, and 150 more were listed as recommended titles.

This section lists and annotates the winning and the honor books. The annotations are a blend of synopsis, classroom application, and analysis of how the title reflects the trends and issues in nonfiction identified in the first five chapters of this book. Finally, each chronological section closes with a bibliography of recommended titles.

The appendix following this section consists of an annotated bibliography of the 2000 Orbis Pictus Award winner, honor books, and recommended titles, which were announced shortly before this book went into production.

1990 Orbis Pictus Award

Fritz, Jean. *The Great Little Madison*. Illustrated with prints and engravings. New York: G. P. Putnam's Sons, 1989. (ISBN: 0-399-21768-1). 159 pp. Ages 10 and up.

Small in stature and smaller in voice, he would exceed even his own expectations in service to his country. Jean Fritz's *The Great Little Madison* offers a well-written and fascinating look at James Madison, fourth president of the United States. Always a quiet presence, Madison's intelligence and unshakable belief in the sovereignty of America led this country through its greatest crisis, that of separation from English rule. Throughout this biography, Fritz impresses the reader with her unlabored and matter-of-fact approach to aspects of Madison's complex personality and political involvements. Conscious of the need to offer her audience background information concerning his upbringing as a prelude to later dramatic decision making, the author succeeds in presenting factual detail without succumbing to the lure of fictionalized dialogue.

The reader gains an appreciation of the virtues of listening as a precursor to public statement and, ultimately, action. When first elected to Congress in 1779, at the age of twenty-nine, the young Madison was a silent presence, but as the country moved closer to conflict with England, he became a vocal proponent for the union of the states. Fritz relates that "James held his tongue for six months and then, whether he could be heard or not, he spoke out . . . . The delegates might strain to hear him, but as time went on, they had to agree that James Madison had sound judgment" (p. 24).

Fritz's descriptions of Madison's interactions with the famous political figures of the times—Thomas Jefferson, the Marquis de Lafayette, Alexander Hamilton, and Patrick Henry, among others—achieve the double purpose of highlighting their historical significance to Madison and the conflict with England, and providing a literary forum for the presentation of different and developing aspects of Madison's character as a man. These relationships, as well as Madison's romance with Dolley Payne Todd, later to become his wife, shed light on Madison's tenacity in pursuit of his convictions.

Fritz's prose is enhanced by accompanying illustrations from period documents, ranging from an example of the secret code developed by Thomas Jefferson and James Madison for privacy purposes, to drawings of the period that depict major players in the American-English conflict and individual episodes of the dramatic saga. The author provides notes as well as a detailed bibliography, which further support her obvious respect for historical research and factual evidence.

1990 Orbis Pictus Honor Books

Blumberg, Rhoda. *The Great American Gold Rush.* Illustrated with period photographs. New York: Bradbury Press, 1989. (ISBN: 0-02-711681-6). 135 pp. Ages 10 and up.

Gold as a psychological magnet and shaper of the dreams and desires of men is center stage in Rhoda Blumberg's *The Great American Gold Rush.* The cover photograph, showing the lone figure of a prospector washing a pan of sand in the hope of finding gold, aptly portrays the dogged determination of men who left ordinary lives in the late nineteenth century in pursuit of dreams of wealth in California. In fascinating descriptions of the early days of discovery, interspersed with details taken from the records of those who traveled to California, Blumberg recreates these exciting and desperate times. Rapidly spreading reports of the discovery caused people from all over the country and even beyond to flock to the site of Sutter's mill. Sutter had been an enterprising, driven man prior to the discovery of gold on his property while he was having a sawmill built. Now he was richer than he had dreamed possible. As the revelation of the find gains impetus, Blumberg's narrative becomes increasingly dramatic. The author examines the individual, local, national, and finally international effects of the discovery. Personal stories are shared, some exhilarating, some heartbreaking.

Blumberg's writing heightens the imagination while also educating the reader about an important event in U.S. history. She makes use of original prints, drawings, maps, and advertisements of the time, impressing the reader with the reality of a situation that at times takes on surreal proportions. Justice was rough and arbitrary: a man could suffer removal of ears, branding, or hanging as a result of attempted gold theft. Blumberg states, "Watching a scaffold being built and witnessing a victim swinging by the neck were often viewed as forms of entertainment" (p. 91), a comment that brings to mind seventeenth-century justice. While contemporary commentators considered the discovery of gold to be indicative of progress, Blumberg points out the regrettable, less positive effects of the find. Disappointed individuals were legion and crime increased, as did a strong distrust of one's neighbor. Secrecy and hoarding were the order of the day.

The author's writing is rich in detail, culminating in stirring statements of the import of the gold rush: "As a result of the Gold Rush, the United States became one of the richest, most powerful nations in the world. Its wealth was measured not only by its gold-filled treasury, but also by its vast, valuable lands that stretched across a continent" (p. 121). Blumberg provides her readers with detailed historical notes, a bibliography, and an index.

Lauber, Patricia. *The News about Dinosaurs.* Illustrated by various artists. New York: Bradbury Press, 1989. (ISBN: 0-02-754520-2). 48 pp. Ages 8–12.

Although prehistoric creatures seem to have an allure of their own, Patricia Lauber's approach to the subject in *The News about Dinosaurs* is informative as well as fascinating. Following a passion for sharing accurate information about important topics established in works such as *Volcano: The Eruption and Healing of Mount St. Helens* (Bradbury Press, 1986), and a desire to make information accessible to a young audience without being condescending, Lauber successfully captures and retains the attention of her readers.

The author takes a three-point approach to the subject of dinosaurs: (1) to examine long-standing beliefs about dinosaur life, (2) to expose inaccurate notions about dinosaurs, and (3) to share new information based on modern research. In so doing, Lauber provides a fresh perspective on the subject. The text is elaborately illustrated using updated artist renderings of what the creatures most likely looked like. These more realistic, yet dramatic visualizations by artist-paleontologists Gregory S. Paul, Douglas Henderson, Mark Hallett, John Gurche, and Robert T. Bakker, in concert with a well-written text, help to dispel ideas that have persisted as a result of earlier, more fanciful artistic approaches.

Lauber's format is visually attractive and appealing. She discusses the newly discovered Baryonyx, Mamenchisaurus, Deinonychus, and Nanotyrannus, as well as their characteristics and eating habits. She highlights recent, more accurate ideas about the life of dinosaurs using an earth-toned caption: "THE NEWS IS." This "announcement" focuses attention on changes in information, allowing the reader to fully appreciate evolving concepts about dinosaur life over time. Knowledge is presented as a constantly evolving dynamic. Lauber underscores the principle that no one can ever claim to have no need for further knowledge; we must be ever alert to new information.

1990 Orbis Pictus Recommended Titles

Adler, David. *We Remember the Holocaust.* New York: Henry Holt, 1989.

Aliki. *The King's Day: Louis XIV of France.* New York: Crowell, 1989.

Ancona, George. *The American Family Farm.* (Text by Joan Anderson.) San Diego: Harcourt, Brace, Jovanovich, 1989.

Calabro, Marian. *Operation Grizzly Bear.* New York: Four Winds Press, 1989.

Hunt, Jonathan. *Illuminations.* New York: Bradbury, 1989.

Jurmain, Suzanne. *Once upon a Horse: A History of Horses and How They Shaped History.* New York: Lothrop, 1989.

Matthews, Downs. *Polar Bear Cubs.* Photographs by Dan Guravich. New York: Simon & Schuster, 1989.

Meltzer, Milton. *Voices from the Civil War: A Documentary History of the Great American Conflict.* New York: Crowell, 1989.

Patent, Dorothy Hinshaw. *Wild Turkey, Tame Turkey.* Photographs by William Muñoz. New York: Clarion, 1989.

Peet, Bill. *Bill Peet: An Autobiography.* Boston: Houghton Mifflin, 1989.

Sills, Leslie. *Inspirations: Stories about Women Artists.* Niles, IL: Albert Whitman, 1989.

Simon, Seymour. *Whales.* New York: Crowell, 1989.

St. George, Judith. *Panama Canal: Gateway to the World.* New York: Putnam, 1989.

1991 Orbis Pictus Award

Freedman, Russell. *Franklin Delano Roosevelt.* New York: Clarion Books, 1990. (ISBN: 0-89919-379-X). 200 pp. Ages 8 and up.

Recognition of and appreciation for individual dynamism and energy are hallmarks of Russell Freedman's thoughtful biography of FDR. Although there is already a wealth of information on the subject of Roosevelt's life and actions in his four terms as president of the United States, it takes the masterful hand of a gifted writer to synthesize the achievements of an individual who dramatically influenced the course of a nation's destiny during the greatest economic and political challenges of the twentieth century.

Freedman's approach is honest. In the chapter "Growing Up Rich," we learn the details of Roosevelt's privileged life. Far from a mere presentation of what it was like to be rich and a Roosevelt, Freedman's discussion is purposeful. The foundation thus laid, the reader appreciates the tremendous change in Roosevelt's character, from slightly arrogant aristocrat to altruistic champion of the rights of the common man. His secretary Frances Perkins, who was later to become the first woman appointed to a presidential cabinet, remarked that Roosevelt's experience of fighting the ravages of poliomyelitis initiated a spiritual transformation in Roosevelt: "The man emerged completely warm hearted, with humility of spirit and with a deeper philosophy. . . . [H]aving been to the depths of trouble, he understood the problems of people in trouble" (p. 56).

While presenting the positives of Roosevelt's career, Freedman does not avoid frank discussion of his weaknesses. He states simply that Roosevelt had a love relationship outside his marriage, and that this circumstance saddened and angered his wife, changing their marriage forever. Freedman suggests that Eleanor's emergence as a strong, outspoken presence was as much a result of her need to compensate for personal unhappiness as it was a desire to pursue humanistic ideals. While emphasizing Roosevelt's bold moves as leader of the nation during the Great Depression and later during World War II, Freedman also points out Roosevelt's failure to act decisively to prevent Hitler from enacting his "final solution." The honest portrayal of positive and negative sides of the subject's character and actions reflects Freedman's respect for his youthful audience. His presentation is never gratuitous, but rather offers an authentic picture of an individual who was overall a "mover and shaker" in U.S. history.

Freedman's text is illustrated liberally with period photographs that capture the spirit of an evolving Roosevelt: as charming young person, mature man, and bold political leader. In addition to a discussion of further sources of information about Roosevelt, Freedman provides an interesting chapter titled "Places to Visit," which offers the audience information on sites central in the life of Roosevelt and his family.

**1991
Orbis Pictus
Honor Books**

Ekoomiak, Normee. *Arctic Memories*. Illustrated by Normee
Ekoomiak. New York: Henry Holt, 1990. (ISBN: 0-8050-2347-X).
Unpaged. Ages 9–12.

In recent years, indigenous people have been increasingly
successful in reclaiming their heritage. Part of this process
includes exercising the right to represent one's own culture
through the media—a means previously controlled by
nonindigenous people. In simple yet stirring prose, Inuit
author-illustrator Normee Ekoomiak shares the story of the
Inuit people of Arctic Quebec. Accompanied by beautifully
detailed miniature drawings and meticulously delicate needle-
work, Ekoomiak creatively communicates to his readers how
the Inuit people live, as well as their hopes and dreams.
Illustrations dominate this presentation, through both size and
brilliancy of color. The essence of the story is told through
illustration, a strategy consistent with cultures more in tune
with orality and visual stimuli. Ekoomiak's text, short and
relatively spare, consists of simply stated facts juxtaposed with
personal recollections and fervent personal beliefs.

Ekoomiak shares several traditional stories that illustrate both
his versatility as an artist and his role as information provider.
In an effort to educate his audience, the author presents the
text in two languages—English and the native Inuktitut—a
further demonstration of authenticity. This approach also
makes the text valuable as a bilingual experience for English-
speakers as well as Inuit young people.

Ekoomiak assists young readers who have no prior experience
with Inuktitut text by providing a discussion of Inuit art and
language, as well as a section titled "Who I Am," in which the
author-illustrator offers more details about himself. *Arctic
Memories* highlights the need for "hearing the voices" of
indigenous people and raises consciousness about the many
ways of sharing information.

Lauber, Patricia. *Seeing Earth from Space*. Photographs by NASA.
New York: Orchard Books, 1990. (ISBN: 0-531-05902-2). 80 pp.
Ages 10 and up.

Versatility and a keen respect for the natural world are evident
in Patricia Lauber's *Seeing Earth from Space*. In clear, informa-
tion-packed prose, Lauber shares the drama of views of the
Earth. Using the advantages of space technology, combined
with reports from those who have traveled through space,
Lauber invites the audience to marvel with her at the many

images that can be captured from space. The photography is breathtaking and certainly must have taken away the breath of the astronauts who first viewed Earth from space.

The author achieves a useful balance between text that discusses what is being viewed—by what means and to what end—and the images themselves. The sheer beauty and size of the photographs dominate the pages, the text often occupying less than a third of the page, and this is an important element of the design. The writing is dense but never overwhelming. Lauber presents a number of terms such as *remote sensing, atoll,* and *spectral signature,* which are probably new to her young audience (and many adults), and discusses these in context with other space vocabulary. The author is always conscious of the reader's need to focus and process.

Lauber has a double message: to share the beauty and wonder that can be accessed through satellite imagery and advanced technology, allowing us to appreciate that "the earth is one planet, small and fragile, wondrous and lovely" (p. 75), and also to offer a rudimentary introduction to how scientists use satellite data. As Lauber states, "Space travelers often return with their thinking changed" (p. 73). This presentation is a valuable learning resource for young people and will help pique their curiosity about an important and expanding technology.

1991 Orbis Pictus Recommended Titles

Alexander, Sally Hobart. *Mom Can't See Me.* Photographs by George Ancona. New York: Macmillan, 1990.

Cole, Joanna. *The Magic School Bus Lost in the Solar System.* Illustrated by Bruce Degen. New York: Scholastic, 1990.

Dowden, Anne Ophelia. *The Clover and the Bee.* New York: Crowell, 1990.

Fisher, Leonard Everett. *The Oregon Trail.* New York: Holiday House, 1990.

Giblin, James Cross. *The Riddle of the Rosetta Stone.* New York: Crowell, 1990.

Hoyt-Goldsmith, Diane. *Totem Pole.* Photographs by Lawrence Migdale. New York: Holiday House, 1990.

Lasky, Kathryn. *Dinosaur Dig.* Photographs by Christopher G. Knight. New York: Morrow Junior Books, 1990.

Lawrence, R. D. *Wolves.* San Francisco/Boston: Sierra Club/Little Brown, 1990.

Levinson, Nancy Smiler. *Christopher Columbus.* New York: Lodestar/Dutton, 1990.

Meltzer, Milton. *Columbus and the World around Him.* New York: Franklin Watts, 1990.

Morimoto, Junko. *My Hiroshima.* New York: Viking, 1990.

Osborne, Mary Pope. *The Many Lives of Benjamin Franklin.* New York: Dial Books for Young Readers, 1990.

Paulsen, Gary. *Wood-Song.* New York: Bradbury, 1990.

Sattler, Helen Roney. *Giraffes.* Illustrated by Christopher Santoro. New York: Lothrop, Lee and Shepard, 1990.

Simon, Seymour. *Oceans.* New York: Morrow Junior Books, 1990.

Stanley, Diane, & Vennema, Peter. *Good Queen Bess.* Illustrated by Diane Stanley. New York: Four Winds Press, 1990.

1992 Orbis Pictus Award

Burleigh, Robert. *Flight: The Journey of Charles Lindbergh.* Illustrated by Mike Wimmer. New York: Philomel Books, 1991. (ISBN: 0-399-22272-3). Unpaged. Ages 5 and up.

Together, Burleigh's prose and Mike Wimmer's vivid impressionistic oil paintings capture the intensity of Charles Lindbergh's remarkable feat of flying solo nonstop from New York to Paris in 1927. The full-color spreads and present-tense narrative keep young readers in suspense for the entire 3,600 miles across the Atlantic—over thirty hours. Readers will ride with the tenacious 25-year-old Lindbergh as he soars in his 5,000-pound airplane, the Spirit of St. Louis.

This book exemplifies the blending of strong narrative style with the dramatic and powerful use in illustrations of color and appropriate highlights. Readers can readily contrast Lindbergh's determined stance in the opening pages with the effects of space, time, and darkness in his cockpit, and then with his dazed acceptance of the celebratory welcome he received in Paris. This picture book biography is highly recommended for the early nonfiction reader. Teachers can help students plot the flight plan on a map of the Atlantic, using posted hours as a time line and monitoring the effects of time and distance on the determination of the young pilot. Readers will quickly learn why Charles Lindbergh became famous overnight.

1992 Orbis Pictus Honor Books

Conrad, Pam. *Prairie Visions: The Life and Times of Solomon Butcher.* Period photographs by Solomon Butcher. New York: HarperCollins, 1991. (ISBN: 0-06-021373-6). 85 pp. Ages 10 and up.

Pam Conrad discovered Solomon Butcher while doing research for her adult novel *Prairie Songs.* The pictures Butcher had taken of Nebraska pioneers were unique because he had photographed families standing before their homesteads with horses and windmills, pianos and cattle. So intrigued was Conrad that she wrote this biographical-historical account of Solomon Butcher who migrated to Nebraska in 1880. Well-documented and presented in album format, the book chronicles the lives of the pioneers who inhabited the turn-of-the-century Nebraska countryside. The narrative and personal photographs knit together the pioneer family tales, as well as the story of Butcher's own life. Inherent in this period piece is an account of the settler's way of life. This book can be used as a reference for students engaged in curricular studies of the westward expansion. The archival photos are a study in themselves, providing young readers insight into the realism captured in each family scene.

Myers, Walter Dean. *Now Is Your Time! The African-American Struggle for Freedom.* Illustrated with period photographs. New York: Harper Trophy, 1991. (ISBN: 0-06-024370-8). 292 pp. Ages 10 and up.

Walter Dean Myers presents a courageous history of the African American struggle for freedom and equality. He begins by setting the scene in America and Europe and then narrates the history, including his own family's, beginning with the capture of the first Africans in 1619. He carefully selects and represents the various perspectives and contributions of significant persons and events, continuing through the American Revolution, the Civil War, and into contemporary times with such landmark events as the legal cases of *Plessy v. Ferguson* and *Brown v. Board of Education.* Woven throughout are the stories of individuals that highlight the dignity of the human spirit. Readers will be inspired by the representative legacies of men and women such as Abd al-Rahman Ibrahima, the well-educated son of a powerful Fula chieftain who was denied his freedom; Thomas Forten, a free African who fought for the freedom of the colonies to help create the United States of America; and Ida B. Wells, a journalist who fought against lynchings and injustices against African Americans. This narrative is well documented, with extensive biographical material and slave narratives. Included are extracts from plantation records, drawings by local artists, and family letters. Central to Myers retelling is his reminder to all young readers that:

> We are a people capable of understanding our own nobility, and our own failures. We have seen who we can be and know that those who have gone before us, who lived their lives well so that we might be free, would demand that we be no less than we can be. An ancient symbol in Ghana is the Sankofa bird. "Sankofa" means to turn back and get what you have left behind. The people of Ghana use it to remind themselves that before you can go forward, you must know where you have been. (p. 274)

This book is recommended for all readers who seek an understanding of their heritage and place in history, and a superb model for personal heritage studies.

1992 Orbis Pictus Recommended Titles

Apfel, Necia H. *Voyager to the Planets.* New York: Clarion Books, 1991.

Blumberg, Rhoda. *The Remarkable Voyages of Captain Cook.* New York: Bradbury Press, 1991.

Freedman, Russell. *The Wright Brothers: How They Invented the Airplane.* Original photographs by Wilbur and Orville Wright. New York: Holiday House, 1991.

Fritz, Jean. *Bully for You, Teddy Roosevelt!* Illustrated by Mike Wimmer. New York: G. P. Putnam's, 1991.

Gelman, Rita Goldman. *Dawn to Dusk in the Galápagos.* Photographs by Tui De Roy. Boston: Little, Brown, 1991.

Greenberg, Jan, & Jordan, Sandra. *The Painter's Eye: Learning to Look at Contemporary American Art.* New York: Delacorte Press, 1991.

Hoyt-Goldsmith, Diana. *Pueblo Storyteller.* New York: Holiday House, 1991.

Keegan, Marcia. *Pueblo Boy: Growing Up in Two Worlds.* New York: Cobblehill Books, 1991.

Lauber, Patricia. *Summer of Fire: Yellowstone 1988.* New York: Orchard Books, 1991.

Maestro, Betsy, & Maestro, Giulio. *The Discovery of the Americas.* New York: Lothrop, Lee and Shepard, 1991.

Pringle, Laurence. *Batman: Exploring the World of Bats.* Photographs by Merlin Tuttle. New York: Charles Scribner's Sons, 1991.

Rylant, Cynthia. *Appalachia: The Voices of Sleeping Birds.* Illustrated by Barry Moser. San Diego: Harcourt, Brace, Jovanovich, 1991.

SanSouci, Robert. *N. C. Wyeth's Pilgrims.* San Francisco: Chronicle Books, 1991.

Simon, Seymour. *Earthquakes.* New York: Morrow Junior Books, 1991.

Zheng, Zhensun, & Low, Alice. *A Young Painter: The Life and Paintings of Wang Yani—China's Extraordinary Young Artist.* New York: Scholastic, 1991.

1993 Orbis Pictus Award

Stanley, Jerry. *Children of the Dust Bowl: The True Story of the School at Weedpatch Camp.* Illustrated with photographs. New York: Crown, 1992. (ISBN: 0-517-58781-5). 85 pp. Ages 10 and up.

Jerry Stanley vividly tells the story of discrimination against children, specifically the offspring of the homeless "Okie" migrant workers who moved from Oklahoma to California during the Great Depression to escape the dust storms. Well documented with authentic black-and-white photographs, this informative and inspirational book on a significant event in U.S. history focuses on the children living in Arvin Federal Camp, an emergency farm-labor camp immortalized in Steinbeck's *The Grapes of Wrath.* In the community of Weedpatch, California, near Bakersfield, the children of the migrant farmworkers were not allowed to attend school. They were ostracized, called "dumb Okies," and went without a school until Leo Hart, a compassionate school superintendent, helped fifty of these children to build their own school. Given the equity issues in today's society and education, this book is highly recommended for all students.

**1993
Orbis Pictus
Honor Books**

Cone, Molly. *Come Back, Salmon: How a Group of Dedicated Kids Adopted Pigeon Creek and Brought It Back to Life.* Photographs by Sidnee Wheelwright. San Francisco: Sierra Club, 1992. (ISBN: 8-87156-572-2). 48 pp. All ages.

This inspirational story describes the efforts of the Jackson Elementary School students in Everett, Washington, to clean up a nearby stream, stock it with salmon, and preserve it as an unpolluted place where the salmon could return to spawn. The simple narrative describes the project and provides background information and dialogue based on interviews with children and teachers.

> "Yuck! What is this, anyway. It looks like a garbage dump to me."
> "No," said Mr. King, "It's a stream. It was a clear clean stream when I was a boy. It was named Pigeon Creek because of all the pigeons nesting around here."
> Students couldn't imagine this muddy, trash-filled gully ever being a stream. (p. 1)

This is a lively, inspiring story of young student scientists in action. The text is highlighted with full-color photographs and informative boxed inserts with details such as: "A salmon sleeps with its eyes open. It has no eyelids." A helpful scientific glossary appears at the end of the book. *Come Back, Salmon* is a great example of documenting a class science project, as well as an exemplar community service project for students. Teachers can use the format to record their own science class inquiries.

Cummings, Pat. *Talking with Artists.* New York: Bradbury Press, 1992. (ISBN: 0-02-724245-5). 96 pp. All ages.

Fourteen distinguished picture book artists talk about their early art experiences, answer questions most frequently asked by children, and offer encouragement to those who would like to become artists. Familiar names included in this collection are Victoria Chess, Pat Cummings, Leo Dillon and Diane Dillon, Richard Egielski, Lois Ehlert, Lisa Campbell Ernst, Tom Feelings, Steven Kellogg, Jerry Pinkney, Amy Schwartz, Lane Smith, Chris Van Allsburg, and David Wiesner. Each section includes an autobiographical summary with photographs of each illustrator as a child and as an adult. A sampling of the artist's early creative efforts is carefully highlighted. For example, Chris Van Allsburg's "Duck-billed Platypus," age 6, is included along with some of his watercolor works from *The Stranger* (Houghton Mifflin, 1986). The presentation also includes advice for the young reader and potential illustrator, and the first-person accounts serve as a model for interviews. Overall, students can use the book as a prototype for their own author-illustrator biographies.

1993 Orbis Pictus Recommended Titles

Brown, Mary Barrett. *Wings along the Waterway.* New York: Orchard Books, 1992.

Freedman, Russell. *An Indian Winter.* Paintings and drawings by Karl Bodmer. New York: Holiday House, 1992.

Gibbons, Gail. *The Great St. Lawrence Seaway.* New York: Morrow Junior Books, 1992.

Harrison, Barbara, & Terris, Daniel. *A Twilight Struggle: The Life of John Fitzgerald Kennedy.* New York: Lothrop, Lee and Shepard, 1992.

Jacobs, Francine. *The Tainos: The People Who Welcomed Columbus.* New York: Putnam, 1992.

Lankford, Mary D. *Hopscotch around the World.* Illustrated by Karen Milone. New York: Morrow Junior Books, 1992.

Lasky, Kathryn. *Surtsey: The Newest Place on Earth.* Photographs by Christopher Knight. New York: Hyperion, 1992.

Meltzer, Milton. *The Amazing Potato.* New York: HarperCollins, 1992.

Murphy, Jim. *The Long Road to Gettysburg.* New York: Clarion Books, 1992.

Pringle, Laurence. *Antarctica.* New York: Simon & Schuster, 1992.

Stanley, Diane, & Vennema, Peter. *Bard of Avon: The Story of William Shakespeare.* New York: Morrow Junior Books, 1992.

1994 Orbis Pictus Award

Murphy, Jim. *Across America on an Emigrant Train.* Illustrated with photographs and prints. New York: Clarion Books, 1992. (ISBN: 0-395-63390-7). 150 pp. Ages 10 and up.

In 1879, Robert Louis Stevenson set off from his home in Scotland and journeyed across the ocean and an entire continent in pursuit of his love and future wife, Fanny Van de Grift Osbourne. Using the narrative thread of Stevenson's journey, Murphy interweaves Stevenson's perceptive account with a thoroughly researched and lively history of the building of the transcontinental railroad. This is history at its best. The book is illustrated with eighty-five archival photographs and line drawings, including maps and detailed captions. Quotes from Stevenson's writings about the trip are frequent.

Across American on an Emigrant Train would well serve any classroom investigation of the transcontinental railroad: how it was planned and built, the roles of different ethnic groups who built it, what it was like to ride it if you were rich and if you were poor, and how it changed the country and those who lived there. The book can also be used for minilessons in reading and writing. Writing lessons might center on descriptive writing, since many quotations reveal Stevenson as a sharp observer. Reading lessons could be of at least two types: (1) Students learning about nonfiction conventions could examine the book, finding endpaper maps, many prints, drawings, carefully captioned black-and-white photographs, and many direct quotations. (2) Another minilesson might focus on sequence. The book relies on chronological order to guide the sequencing of information. Students can identify each year, or period of years, that serves as a backdrop for each chapter. Working together, they might even develop a time line, which would help them see why Murphy purposefully presented his information in a linear sequence.

1994 Orbis Pictus Honor Books

Brandenburg, Jim. *To the Top of the World: Adventures with Arctic Wolves.* Edited by Joann Bren Guernsey. Illustrated with photographs. New York: Walker, 1993. (ISBN: 0-8027-8219-1). 44 pp. All ages.

This compelling and highly personal photo-essay about the Arctic wolf chronicles Brandenburg's months spent with a wolf pack on Ellsmere Island in the Northwest Territories. The book is both breathtaking and profound. Through close-up photographs that only a dedicated and daring photojournalist could capture, Jim Brandenburg brings his passion and expertise to the page for children. Organized by Brandenburg's encounters, the chapters cover his first glimpse of an Arctic wolf (where he takes the "picture of his life"), his meeting and living with "the family" of wolves, his exploration into how wolves adapt and hunt, and finally his philosophical positions and goodbyes. What might strike the young reader most is the chasm Brandenburg helps create between what the world thinks it knows about wolves—that they are extremely dangerous, for example—and what is actually known. By book's end, awe replaces the myths.

Brandenburg's enthusiasm for his subject matter; his willing-
ness to risk his life for a picture; his clear, well-paced writing
style; and his great respect for young readers all set this book
apart. Describing an encounter that almost cost his life, for
example, Brandenburg writes: "I hesitate to dwell on this
episode because wolves already have a bad enough reputation. . . . Thanks in part to movies and books, the mere sound
of a wolf howling in the distance is often enough to inspire
terror" (p. 41). Young readers, however, are never terrified.
Exceptional photography will help them see the tenderness of
this species, its intelligence, and its family-oriented, loving
behavior.

This book can be used in conjunction with Seymour Simon's
Wolves (HarperCollins, 1993), which explores North American
wolves' physical characteristics, habits, and natural environment. To learn more about other animals that live in the Arctic,
in particular at the Arctic National Wildlife Refuge, examine
Karen Panell's *Land of Dark, Land of Light* (Dutton, 1993). Like
Brandenburg's book, this text acquaints readers with information on how animals adapt and live in the harsh climate. To
these, add Stephen Swinburne's *Once a Wolf: How Wildlife
Biologists Fought to Bring Back the Gray Wolf* (Houghton Mifflin,
1999), an important photo-essay showing the efforts of dedicated scientists to prevent the extinction of the much-maligned
wolf.

Brooks, Bruce. *Making Sense: Animal Perception and Communication.*
    New York: Farrar, Straus and Giroux, 1993. (ISBN: 0-374-
    34742-5). 74 pp. Ages 8–13.

Bruce Brooks explores the six senses—seeing, hearing, smell-
ing, tasting, touching, and feeling—of various animals, and
then takes the reader a step further to the more subtle sense of
awareness that comes when the six are put together. Because
humans are more than a combination of the basic senses,
Brooks challenges the reader to explore the boundary between
quantifiable behavior and animal feelings: "dare we insist that
. . . the dog just rebuffed by its cranky master is not sad?" (p. 67).

Making Sense is the third volume in the author's award-winning Knowing Nature series, and perhaps his stylistic best. It
opens with an engaging, personal story about snorkeling, told
with great suspense: "One second I was slipping effortlessly
through liquid crystal; the next second I was stuck inside a
thick silver mass that pulsated on every side with the current"
(p. 1). He uses an informal, lighthearted tone to teach and

amuse. When writing about color, for instance, we hear Brooks's distinctive voice: "Higher visibility—despite certain obvious drawbacks when it comes to lying low—is almost always perceived as a kind of power, completely desirable or enviable to members of the same species" (p. 13). Full-color, well-placed photographs appear throughout the book, clearly illustrating details of animal anatomy. Unfortunately, the information is not sourced, an omission that, toward the end of the 1990s, might have prevented this title from being an honor book.

Because this book's power is its focus on wholeness, it should be read aloud and discussed. The issues are mighty and complex. For example, will students question Brooks as he explores the boundary between animal behavior and feelings? Brooks's mind is open. How do students come to understand what Brooks means when he asks, "dare we insist?" Because shared books coupled with class discussion often lead to the exploration of related texts, teachers might introduce Jim Brandenburg's *To the Top of the World: Adventures with Arctic Wolves* (Walker, 1993), which explores boundaries as well.

1994 Orbis Pictus Recommended Titles

Bash, Barbara. *Shadows of Night: The Hidden World of the Little Brown Bat.* San Francisco: Sierra Club Books, 1993.

Carrick, Carol. *Whaling Days.* Woodcuts by David Frampton. New York: Clarion Books, 1993.

Freedman, Russell. *Eleanor Roosevelt: A Life of Discovery.* New York: Clarion Books, 1993.

Giblin, James Cross. *Be Seated: A Book about Chairs.* New York: HarperCollins, 1993.

Hamilton, Virginia. *Many Thousand Gone: African Americans from Slavery to Freedom.* Illustrated by Leo and Diane Dillon. New York: Knopf, 1993.

Knight, Amelia Stewart. *The Way West: Journal of a Pioneer Woman.* Pictures by Michael McCurdy. New York: Simon & Schuster, 1993.

Lawrence, Jacob. *The Great Migration: An American Story.* New York: HarperCollins, 1993.

Meltzer, Milton. *Lincoln: In His Own Words.* Illustrated by Stephen Alcorn. San Diego: Harcourt Brace, 1993.

Moser, Barry. *Fly! A Brief History of Flight Illustrated.* New York: HarperCollins, 1993.

Pinkney, Andrea Davis. *Seven Candles for Kwanzaa.* Pictures by Brian Pinkney. New York: Dial Books, 1993.

Toll, Nelly S. *Behind the Secret Window: A Memoir of a Hidden Childhood during World War Two.* New York: Dial Books, 1993.

van der Rol, Ruud, & Verhoeven, Rian. *Anne Frank: Beyond the Diary.* New York: Viking Press, 1993.

**1995
Orbis Pictus
Award**

Swanson, Diane. *Safari beneath the Sea: The Wonder World of the North Pacific Coast.* Photographs by the Royal British Columbia Museum. San Francisco: Sierra Club Books for Children, 1994. (ISBN: 0-87156-415-7). 64 pp. Ages 8–12.

Because of winds, currents, and geography, the coastal water of the North Pacific between Alaska and Oregon lends itself to exciting exploration. This is precisely what Diane Swanson documents in her award-winning text. Large, outstandingly crisp color photos tell the story of the strange habits of familiar creatures, such as the octopus (which she compares to a cat) and the slug, as well as the family life, eating habits, and self-preservation techniques of lesser-known fish, including the lingcod, hagfish, warbonnet, and more. The narrative is easy to understand, clear, and poetic.

With consistency across chapters, Swanson uses a variety of access features such as sidebars and bulleted lists, which means that the book does not necessarily have to be read from cover to cover. Teachers might take advantage of this aspect of the book to explore other texts with similar features. They might read aloud a chapter of *Safari beneath the Sea,* calling attention to the nonfiction conventions and exploring how the headings, sidebars, bullets, captions, and photographs work together. Then children might examine other chapters to test for consistency. This book could be read as part of an ocean study unit, along with related titles such as *Coral Reefs: Earth's Undersea Treasures* by Laurence Pringle (Simon & Schuster, 1992) and *Deep-Sea Vents: Living World without Sun* by John F. Waters (Cobblehill, 1994).

**1995
Orbis Pictus
Honor Books**

Dewey, Jennifer Owings. *Wildlife Rescue: The Work of Dr. Kathleen Ramsay.* Photographs by Don MacCarter. Honesdale, PA: Boyds Mills Press, 1994. (ISBN: 0-56397-045-7). 64 pp. Ages 7 and up.

This book focuses on the rescue work of veterinarian Kathleen Ramsay as she performs surgery and encourages the recuperation of her animal patients. In four gripping chapters, Dewey explores the challenges faced by Ramsay and her dedicated staff at the Wildlife Center in Espanola, New Mexico. Their practice is unusual: reattaching a toad's tongue; feeding a hummingbird nestling a soup of chopped eggs, baby food meat, and mashed insects; repairing a fractured hawk leg. While the life-and-death stories of specific injured animals serve to capture the young reader's attention, the reader never loses sight of the larger issue of wildlife rehabilitation. Dewey reports Ramsay's belief that an animal born wild has the right to live and die that way. Ramsay and her staff's every gesture and act work toward "Return to the Wild," the title of the book's last chapter.

Dewey first captures the intensity of Dr. Ramsay's work through the story of a family out for a walk. Without warning they are in the throes of disaster: their dog is attacked by a wild beaver; one of the children is threatened; the mother hits the beaver over the head, killing it; and two beaver kits have to be flown to Ramsay's Wildlife Center. Smooth writing and straightforward language keep the young reader a true participant: "Lynne and Dr. Ramsay understand each other. Often they work side-by-side, pinning a broken wing bone or stitching a wound. They work under great stress and to the point of exhaustion" (p. l6). Sharp color photos with easy-to-understand captions document the work of the center and capture the strong emotions felt by the staff.

Further study could include learning about similar local centers that care for wild animals. Visits with veterinarians and wildlife managers can extend students' understanding of the complexity of caring for ill or injured wild animals. In addition, teachers might consult *Care of the Wild Feathered & Furred: Treating and Feeding Injured Birds and Animals* by Mae Hickman, Maxine Guy, and Stephen Levine (Coyote Moon, 1998). This book is a guide to caring for an ill or injured wild animal until it is in the capable hands of a doctor such as Ramsay.

Freedman, Russell. *Kids at Work: Lewis Hine and the Crusade against Child Labor.* Illustrated with photographs by Lewis Hine. New York: Clarion Books, 1994. (ISBN: 0-395-58703-4). 104 pp. Ages 8–12.

This remarkable biography of Lewis Hine explores the crusade against child labor. The narrative tracks Hine's life from his work as a hauler in an Oshkosh furniture factory, to teacher, to photographer, a photographer who will one day perch himself on a mooring mast atop the Empire State Building to get a special shot. Hine risked his life more than once to capture on film the torture children had to endure as laborers—breaker boys, spinners, glass factory workers, farmhands, glass blowers, shrimp pickers—in the early twentieth century. Working for the National Child Labor Committee, Hine took photographs that appeared in newspapers, in magazines, and in a steady stream of publications generated by the committee. Freedman deftly incorporates a variety of historical sources, including a Birmingham, Alabama, reporter who wrote about a Hine exhibit: "There has been no more convincing proof of the absolute necessity of child labor laws . . . than these pictures showing the suffering, the degradation, the immoral influence, the utter lack of anything that is wholesome in the lives of these poor little wage earners" (p. 72).

Freedman does an outstanding job of presenting the facts of Lewis Hine's crusade. Students view authentic Hine photographs and read quotations based on factual accounts and letters, all listed in the extensive bibliography. The attractive format and photographs complement quality prose, which is filled with authentic dialogue, well-selected quotes, and fascinating anecdotes. Classroom teachers in grades 4 and up can recommend this volume to students seeking biographies steeped in context, histories that span a time period, information on the evolution of child labor laws, or examples of good photo-histories. The book is decidedly nonfrenetic, a welcome relief from more modern page layouts that often force the eye everywhere at once.

McKissack, Patricia C., & McKissack, Fredrick L. *Christmas in the Big House, Christmas in the Quarters.* Illustrated by John Thompson. New York: Scholastic, 1994. (ISBN: 0-590-43027-0). 68 pp. Ages 8 and up.

Readers are asked to become time travelers in this detailed description of Christmas traditions on a Southern plantation just prior to the Civil War. The year is 1859; the place is Virginia. Through meticulous research, the authors contrast life in the plantation mansion with life in the slave quarters, not in one specific setting but in a composite setting woven by the McKissacks. Readers see and feel the elegance and beauty of the big house, as well as the cramped, one-room, dirt floor cabins of the slave quarters. Whereas authentically written conversations about John Brown's raid, slave insurrection, secession, and possible war typify the concerns of occupants of the big house, conversations about freedom dominate talk in the quarters. The holiday celebration of 1859 marked the end of an era that is now remembered in songs, poems, and rituals, many of which appear in the book.

This book could be used as the centerpiece in a debate on the issue of intermingling fact and fiction. The McKissacks include a foreword stating that while the conversation, dialogue, and setting are authentic, events are condensed and relocated to help the story flow. In addition, thanks to careful research the authors have created a plausible scenario—another way contemporary authors bridge the divide between fiction and nonfiction. For comparison purposes, teachers might share books such as *Slave Young, Slave Long: The American Slave Experience* by Meg Green (Lerner, 1999). Pairs of students might explore the book's compare-and-contrast format, with one reading aloud chapters about the big house and another reading those about the slave quarters, then both discussing the authors' choice of this organizational structure.

1995 Orbis Pictus Recommended Titles

Bash, Barbara. *Ancient Ones: The World of the Old-Growth Douglas Fir.* San Francisco: Sierra Club Books, 1994.

Busenberg, Bonnie. *Vanilla, Chocolate, & Strawberry: The Story of Your Favorite Flavors.* Minneapolis: Lerner, 1994.

Calmenson, Stephanie. *Rosie, a Visiting Dog's Story.* Photographs by Justin Sutcliffe. New York: Clarion Books, 1994.

Davidson, Rosemary. *Take a Look: An Introduction to the Experience of Art.* New York: Viking, 1994.

George, Jean Craighead. *Animals Who Have Won Our Hearts.* Illustrated by Christine Herman Merrill. New York: HarperCollins, 1994.

Krull, Kathleen. *Lives of Writers: Comedies, Tragedies (and What the Neighbors Thought).* Illustrated by Kathryn Hewitt. San Diego: Harcourt Brace, 1994.

Lauber, Patricia. *Fur, Feathers, and Flippers: How Animals Live Where They Do.* New York: Scholastic, 1994.

Luenn, Nancy. *Squish! A Wetland Walk.* New York: Atheneum, 1994.

Markle, Sandra. *Science to the Rescue.* New York: Atheneum, 1994.

Marrin, Albert. *Unconditional Surrender: U. S. Grant and the Civil War.* New York: Atheneum, 1994.

Meltzer, Milton. *Cheap Raw Material.* New York: Viking, 1994.

Monceaux, Morgan. *Jazz: My Music, My People.* New York: Knopf, 1994.

Stanley, Diane, & Vennema, Peter. *Cleopatra.* New York: Morrow, 1994.

Stanley, Jerry. *I Am an American.* New York: Crown, 1994.

**1996
Orbis Pictus
Award**

Murphy, Jim. *The Great Fire.* New York: Scholastic, 1995. (ISBN: 0-590-47267-4). 144 pp. Ages 10 and up.

A read-aloud for younger students and a read-alone for the upper grades and beyond, *The Great Fire* debunks over a century of myths about the fire that began in the O'Leary barn on October 8, 1871, forcing 100,000 Chicagoans to flee their homes. Readers experience the fire thanks to many eyewitness accounts culled from books, newspapers, magazines, and letters, but they view it most intimately through the eyes of four survivors: a 21-year-old reporter, a newspaper editor, a visitor to the city, and a 12-year-old resident. The origins of the fire, missteps in fighting it, and efforts to rebuild the city in the aftermath come alive in a blend of historical facts and personal accounts. As in a good novel, children will become absorbed from the start in captivating details: "It was Sunday and an unusually warm evening for October eighth, so Daniel 'Peg Leg' Sullivan left his stifling little house in the West Side of Chicago and went to visit neighbors. One of his stops was at the shingled cottage of Patrick and Catherine O'Leary" (p. 13). But this is not a novel; it is pure fact, gleaned from thorough research that is on display not only in the text but also in an inviting design that includes varied graphics: reproductions of carefully selected documents, period drawings, newspaper clippings, archival photographs, and double-spread maps revealing the location and scope of the destruction.

Murphy's earlier historical photo-essays, including *The Boys' War* (Clarion, 1990), *The Long Road to Gettysburg* (Clarion, 1992), and *Across America on an Emigrant Train* (Clarion, 1993; winner of the 1994 Orbis Pictus Award) are ample evidence that history in the hands of an artistic and passionate researcher and writer is anything but boring.

1996 Orbis Pictus Honor Books

Colman, Penny. *Rosie the Riveter: Women Working on the Home Front in World War II.* New York: Crown, 1995. (ISBN: 0-517-59790-X, trade / 0-517-59791-8, library). 120 pp. Ages 10 and up.

With a spotlight on one young girl named Dot Chastney, Colman brings the years 1942–1945 to life from a child's perspective. The book is, at once, a thoughtful examination of the United States during World War II, of the wartime workplace, and of women's history: the jobs women held, the impact women had on the workplace, and the fate of women at war's end. It is an insightful commentary on evolving attitudes about the role of women in U.S. society. Colman's narrative style, distinguished by its clarity, is built on a foundation of abundant primary source material including, for example, interview transcripts and quotations from period magazines. Complementing the text are well-placed black-and-white photos and posters illustrating women working in traditional male occupations, part of the public relations campaign that lured them there. Also included are a chronology and a bibliography.

Middle school students might use *Rosie the Riveter* as a starting point for exploring the roles of women in times of war in this country. Even during the American Revolution women were participants. Betty Hager, for example, was at the scene of the first battle at Concord, Massachusetts, where she used her blacksmithing skills to repair cannons used against the British. Hundreds of women served as camp followers, trailing soldiers on long marches, staying in their camps to cook, taking care of the sick and wounded, and mending clothes. During the Civil War, women ran farms when their men left for battle. Other women were scouts, spies, and soldiers. Additionally, *Rosie the Riveter* might accompany texts that explore women's rights and/or civil rights.

Pringle, Laurence. *Dolphin Man: Exploring the World of Dolphins.*
      Photographs by Randall S. Wells and the Dolphin Biology
      Research Institute. New York: Atheneum, 1995. (ISBN: 0-689-
      80299-4), 42 pp. Ages 9–13.

Dolphin Man is not just another book about dolphins, but a
photo-biography of one of the world's foremost experts on
dolphins, Randy Wells. Pringle, a biologist himself, paints a
fascinating portrait of this marine biologist and invites a close-
up look at the subject of his study: bottlenose dolphins. Pringle
has masterfully pulled together fact and biography, demonstrating that good nonfiction can weave fact and narrative in
powerful ways. He integrates Randy's story of tracking,
observing, even hanging out with individual dolphins, with
facts about dolphin behavior: how they live together, mate,
raise their young, fight predators, and communicate. The facts
and photographs are well documented, not only by Randy
Wells, but also by the Dolphin Biology Research Institute.
Picture captions are clear and perfectly placed.

For children, the eye-opening chapter "Growing Up in a
Dolphin Community" explains how scientists identify dolphins and clearly foreshadows the interactivity we see nowadays in good nonfiction. Patterns of nicks and notches on the
dolphins, combined with information gained by catching
dolphins, enable Randy and other researchers to learn about
the Sarasota Bay dolphin community. In an effort to emulate
what Randy does, students might be given small, identical
paper dolphin fins and, with a realistic explanation in mind,
add their own "nicks and notches." Students could then hear
each other's stories, followed by "identifying" each other's
dolphins.

Dolphin Man dovetails nicely with Steve Parker's *Whales and
Dolphins* (Sierra Club, 1994) and Marcia Segilson and George
Ancona's *Dolphins at Grassy Key* (Macmillan, 1989). Consider
also Madeleine L'Engle's novel *A Ring of Endless Light* (Farrar,
Straus and Giroux, 1980) for stronger readers, Nathaniel
Benchley's easy-to-read book *Several Tricks of Edgar Dolphin*
(HarperCollins, 1970), and Wayne Grover's *Dolphin Adventure:
A True Story* (Greenwillow, 1990).

**1996
Orbis Pictus
Recommended
Titles**

Bial, Raymond. *The Underground Railroad.* Boston: Houghton Mifflin, 1995.

Fraser, Mary Ann. *In Search of the Grand Canyon.* New York: Henry Holt, 1995.

George, Jean Craighead. *Everglades.* Paintings by Wendell Minor. New York: HarperCollins, 1995.

Giblin, James Cross. *When Plague Strikes.* New York: HarperCollins, 1995.

Johnson, Sylvia. *Raptor Rescue!* Photographs by Ron Winch. New York: Dutton, 1995.

Keeler, Patricia A., & McCall Jr., Francis X. *Unraveling Fibers.* New York: Atheneum, 1995.

McMahon, Patricia. *Listen for the Bus.* Photographs by John Godt. Honesdale, PA: Boyds Mills Press, 1995.

McMillan, Bruce. *Summer Ice: Life along the Antarctic Peninsula.* Boston: Houghton Mifflin, 1995.

Micucci, Charles. *The Life and Times of the Honeybee.* Boston: Houghton Mifflin, 1995.

Pandell, Karen, with Bryant, Barry. *Learning from the Dalai Lama.* Photographs by John B. Taylor. New York: Dutton, 1995.

Pringle, Laurence. *Fire in the Forest.* Paintings by Bob Marstall. New York: Atheneum, 1995.

Robbins, Ken. *Air.* New York: Henry Holt, 1995.

Sattler, Helen Roney. *The Book of North American Owls.* Illustrated by Jean Day Zallinger. New York: Clarion Books, 1995.

Switzer, Ellen. 1995. *The Magic of Mozart.* Photographs by Costas. New York: Atheneum, 1995.

Waldman, Neil. *The Golden City.* New York: Atheneum, 1995.

**1997
Orbis Pictus
Award**

Stanley, Diane. *Leonardo da Vinci.* New York: Morrow Junior Books, 1996. (ISBN: 0-688-10437-1, trade / 0-688-10438-X, library). 48 pp. (unpaged). Ages 8 and up.

This breathtakingly beautiful biography of Leonardo da Vinci, the Italian Renaissance artist and inventor, describes his life, art, inventions, and explorations into the unknown. Stanley illustrates the book in the style of the old masters and follows the life of da Vinci from his baptism to his deathbed. To provide context for a young audience, she includes an introduction to the Italian Renaissance. The full-page illustrations detail da Vinci's world—the rural setting where he spent his early years, the artist's studio where he served as an apprentice, the court of his first patron, and the churches that housed some of his most influential artwork. Reproductions from da Vinci's famous notebooks provide further evidence of his inventive mind and of his careful study and understanding of nature, anatomy, flight, weaponry, and more. These vivid drawings, chosen to reflect ideas and events in the story, juxtapose well with Stanley's large paintings.

In the classroom, teachers will want to point out how authors address interpretation and/or unknown information. As in her other nonfiction titles, Stanley is eager to note that parts of da Vinci's life remain a mystery and that historical interpretation is a continuous process. For example, the art historian Giorgio Vasari told of how da Vinci died in the arms of Francis I. This account is discredited years later by a French scholar and then restored as fact later on. The use of da Vinci's original notebooks to extend the narrative provides young writers with a model both for how to use primary sources in their own work and how they might record their own original ideas.

1997 Orbis Pictus Honor Books

Blumberg, Rhoda. *Full Steam Ahead: The Race to Build a Transcontinental Railroad.* Washington, DC: National Geographic Society, 1996. (ISBN: 0-7922-2715-8). 160 pp. Ages 9 and up.

Influenced by the public feeling of manifest destiny, the gold rush, the sluggishness of commerce, and the Civil War, Americans came to realize that a link between eastern and western United States was vital. Thus came The Pacific Railroad Act of 1862, and right along with it a race between the Central Pacific and Union Pacific Railroads. One company was to start from the outskirts of Sacramento, the other from the Mississippi River. Victory was awarded to the company that could get to the California border first: that company could keep building. In ten well-paced chapters, with plenty of photographs, enlarged engravings, maps, and footnotes to augment the text, Blumberg brings the challenge, and ultimately the accomplishment, to life. She immediately uncovers the intricacies of sleazy business deals and illuminates stupid decisions, then moves on to detail raucous, railroad-town life, portray the remarkable perseverance of the Chinese and Native American laborers who did the work, and celebrate the brilliance of great engineering. What a ride. Teachers will be pleased that even reluctant readers enjoy the book.

Freedman, Russell. *The Life and Death of Crazy Horse.* Illustrated with pictographs by Amos Bad Heart Bull. New York: Holiday House, 1996. (ISBN: 0-8234-1219-9). 166 pp. Ages 10 and up.

This is a carefully researched and balanced account of Crazy Horse, the legendary Lakota Sioux leader whose short life has come to personify the struggles of the Lakota Sioux during the last half of the 1800s. By Crazy Horse's time, a new wave of migrants was beginning to sweep westward. Confronted with a powerful threat to their hunting grounds and freedom, the Sioux, like other tribes, fought back. Freedman depicts Crazy Horse as a classic hero driven by both vision and grace, and helps the reader understand his stubborn resistance to the war's changing tide. He couples his text with the concrete details of fifty black-and-white pictographs drawn by a tribal historian.

Freedman's story of Crazy Horse is as significant today as any historical account, wars between the oppressor and the oppressed always good material for encouraging deeper student understanding and enlightenment, particularly when the story is well told. Freedman's sense of timing and level of detail are impeccable. He knows his young audience and understands that they will want to know not only about Crazy Horse's driving vision and courage, but also about his loves and tender nature. The issue of source documentation is always a concern in histories of people whose past is captured by oral or pictorial traditions. Freedman had access to Eleanor Hinman and Mari Sandoz's interviews of Crazy Horse's surviving friends and relatives, noting that their stories "did not often disagree" (p. 3). The accidental find by graduate student Helen Blish of the ledger sketchbook kept by Amos Bad Heart Bull enriches Freedman's text.

In the classroom, *The Life and Death of Crazy Horse* could prove to be a riveting reading event if the teacher encourages its reading as a starting point to making connections across time and cultures. Many connections might be made, from the personality often associated with Alexander the Great to

Shakespeare's tenderhearted, lovesick Romeo. The book might be combined with other accounts of Crazy Horse, such as Judith St. George's *Crazy Horse* (Putnam, 1994), as well as with books depicting the trauma of westward expansion on all Native American tribes.

Osborne, Mary Pope. *One World, Many Religions: The Ways We Worship.* New York: Knopf, 1996. (ISBN: 0-679-83930-5, trade / 0-679-93930-X, library). 86 pp. Ages 10 and up.

In six readable chapters about the world's major religions—Judaism, Christianity, Islam, Hinduism, Buddhism, and Confucianism/Taoism—Osborne introduces readers to religious history, beliefs, and practices. Her prose is balanced and concise, informative and engrossing, accessible and thoughtful. Both black-and-white and color photographs depict religious images as well as children and adults around the world engaged in worship. Aids for readers include a table of contents, a glossary, a world map showing where various religions are practiced, seven time lines, a bibliography, and an index. A brief introduction explores the purpose of religion, the meaning of the word, religious history, and the impact of religion on life. It concludes with a unifying theme:

> Although these seven religions have different beliefs and teach different ways to worship, they have certain important things in common:
> They all seek to comfort their followers.
> They all offer thanks for the world's great beauty and goodness.
> They all express awe and humility before the mysteries of the universe.
> In this sense, they are all wise and enduring. (p. ix)

This handsomely designed volume has no peer as a fine review for adults, an introduction for children, and an invitation to all for further in-depth study of particular religious traditions.

1997 Orbis Pictus Recommended Titles

Arnosky, Jim. *Nearer Nature.* New York: Lothrop, 1996.

Ashabranner, Brent. *A Strange and Distant Shore: Indians of the Great Plains in Exile.* New York: Cobblehill Books, 1996.

Bartoletti, Susan Campbell. *Growing Up in Coal Country.* Boston: Houghton Mifflin, 1996.

Bial, Raymond. *With Needle and Thread: A Book about Quilts*. Boston: Houghton Mifflin, 1996.

Cha, Dia. *Dia's Story Cloth: The Hmong People's Journey of Freedom*. Stitched by Chue and Nhia Thao Cha. New York: Lee and Low/ Denver Museum of Natural History, 1996.

Cooper, Floyd. *Mandela: From the Life of the South African Statesman*. New York: Philomel, 1996.

Fleischman, Sid. *The Abracadabra Kid: A Writer's Life*. New York: Greenwillow Press, 1996.

Fradin, Dennis Brindell. *"We Have Conquered Pain": The Discovery of Anesthesia*. New York: McElderry/Simon & Schuster, 1996.

Jaffe, Steven H. *Who Were the Founding Fathers? Two Hundred Years of Reinventing American History*. New York: Henry Holt, 1996.

Lauber, Patricia. *Hurricanes: Earth's Mightiest Storms*. New York: Scholastic, 1996.

Osofsky, Audrey. *Free to Dream: The Making of a Poet: Langston Hughes*. New York: Lothrop, Lee and Shepard, 1996.

Reef, Catherine. *John Steinbeck*. New York: Clarion Books, 1996.

Sis, Peter. *Starry Messenger: A Book Depicting the Life of a Famous Scientist, Mathematician, Astronomer, Philosopher, Physician, Galileo Galilei*. New York: Farrar, Straus and Giroux, 1996.

Wright-Frierson, Virginia. *A Desert Scrapbook: Dawn to Dusk in the Sonoran Desert*. New York: Simon & Schuster, 1996.

1998 Orbis Pictus Award

Pringle, Laurence. *An Extraordinary Life: The Story of a Monarch Butterfly*. Illustrated with paintings by Bob Marstall. New York: Orchard Books, 1997. (ISBN: 0-531-30002-1, trade / 0-531-33002-8, library). 64 pp. Ages 9 and up.

This beautifully designed life cycle book uses the most current research on *Danaus plexippus*, the northern milkweed-eating monarch butterfly, to explore its development, its migration, and the perils in its survival. Through a clever narrative, in which Pringle engages the reader by naming and following just one butterfly, readers learn about the intricacies of this small creature's struggle to survive. Colorful illustrations by landscape painter Bob Marstall provide illuminating perspectives on the monarch's development and anatomy as well as its food sources and natural predators. While Pringle walks close to the anthropomorphic line with his naming technique, he manages not to cross it by depending on information and feedback from monarch experts.

Migration maps and informative sidebars—which depict a wealth of interconnections with other animals, geography, people, climate, and history—provide many classroom opportunities for learning and exploration. Teachers will want to walk students through the sidebars, helping them to notice and understand how they extend meaning. The book is also a good example of how authors may deftly use context, typographic features, and visuals to define words. Students who work well independently have much to explore, from monarch myths to mathematical patterns found on monarch wings. Other students might find and draw food chains; research the current debate on choosing the national insect of the United States; or become involved with Monarch Watch, a group trying to solve the mysteries of monarch migration. Students who follow specific authors may explore other Pringle-Marstall collaborations by comparing *An Extraordinary Life* to *Fire in the Forest: A Cycle of Growth and Renewal* (Atheneum, 1995), and their recent collaboration, *A Dragon in the Sky: The Story of a Green Darner Dragonfly* (Orchard, 2001).

1998 Orbis Pictus Honor Books

Dorros, Arthur. *A Tree Is Growing.* Illustrated by S. D. Schindler. New York: Scholastic, 1997. (ISBN: 0-590-45300-9). 32 pp. Ages 7 and up.

This uniquely illustrated book for young children is an introduction to trees. Following the growth of the noble oak over the course of a year, Dorros describes the structure of trees, how they grow, and their uses. The full-page illustrations captivate—they are textured, etched on parchment and pastel papers, and filled in with colored pencil, conveying the subtle textures of bark and leaves. Because of the glorious illustrations, the reader is drawn deeply into the text and the informative sidebars, which explain complex processes such as photosynthesis, or provide interesting details such as how a baobab tree stores water. The poetic language is both imaginative and joyful. The primary text uses simple analogies (roots are like pipelines) and hooks the young reader by encouraging a transaction between the reader and the text: "Bark is the skin of a tree. The outer layer of bark protects the tree. When an oak tree is young, the bark is as smooth as a baby's skin" (unpaged).

Possibilities for classroom activities abound for readers of all ages. Teachers will find it a perfect read-aloud because of its inquisitive and predictive nature, inviting illustrations, and potential use as a model for effective sidebars. Because the drawings are labeled and full of facts, science students will want to pour over the details on their own. *My Favorite Tree: Terrific Trees of North America* by Diane Iverson (Dawn, 1999) would prove a good companion piece. A tree lover's book, this small paperback details specific gifts trees give to children while tracing historic uses by Native Americans, colonial settlers, and pioneers of the westward movement.

Giblin, James Cross. *Charles Lindbergh: A Human Hero.* New York: Clarion Books, 1997. (ISBN: 0-395-63389-3). 212 pp. Ages 10 and up.

In this sympathetic and well-documented introduction to Charles Lindbergh, Giblin humanizes his subject by presenting flaws as well as accomplishments. He reveals Lindbergh's Nazi sympathies in an evenhanded manner, giving the reader a sense of the complete man—a man he calls "an all-too-human hero." The text is meticulously researched and includes a generous selection of archival photos. One leaves the text feeling that Lindbergh earned his place in aviation history. There is much to admire in the careful approach Giblin takes as he writes for young adults. The book opens with a full-page photograph of the *Spirit of St. Louis,* followed by text that carefully situates the young reader:

> They're all there in the central hall of the National Air and Space Museum in Washington, D.C. The 1903 Flyer in which the Wright Brothers made the first successful heavier-than-air flight. The 1962 Mercury spacecraft in which John Glenn became the first American to orbit the earth. And the Apollo 11 command module that carried Neil Armstrong, Edwin Aldrin Jr., and Michael Collins to the moon and back in July 1969.
>   Above them all, hanging from the ceiling on wires, is what looks at first glance like just another old, small plane. (p. 1)

An extensive index, source notes, and chronology make Giblin's book a useful reference tool. This volume could be used in conjunction with Barry Denenberg's biography *An American Hero: The True Story of Charles A. Lindbergh* (Scholastic, 1996). Exploring the differences in the authors' perspectives and approaches could foster students' critical reading and writing. The 1993 Orbis Pictus winner, *Flight: The Journey of Charles Lindbergh,* by Robert Burleigh, a picture book that covers Lindbergh's transatlantic flight, might also be shared.

Hampton, Wilborn. *Kennedy Assassinated! The World Mourns: A Reporter's Story.* Cambridge, MA: Candlewick, 1997. (ISBN: 1-56402-811-9). 96 pp. Ages 10 and up.

President John F. Kennedy's assassination and its shocking aftermath are chronicled step-by-step by Hampton, who on November 22, 1963, was a recent college graduate and a rookie reporter for United Press International. He takes the reader along with him as he narrates events, beginning with a report of gunfire, through Lee Harvey Oswald's death and Kennedy's funeral. In an epilogue, Hampton reflects on the import of those days to the country and to his own journalistic career:

> Since then I have covered many big stories, from wars and riots to summit meetings and world conferences, from hijackings and coups to international sporting championships and even other assassinations.
>
> But it soon became clear to me that no matter how many front-page stories I covered or how many Bulletins I wrote, I had covered the biggest story of my life on November 22, 1963, and that nothing I did later would ever be quite the same. (p. 89)

Kennedy Assassinated! is riveting not only because of its auto-biographical element but also because of its superbly complementary design and illustrations, including endpapers composed of a collage of news clippings, an abundance of black-and-white news photographs, reproductions of pertinent documents, and margin photos of major players. Hampton's account of his role in a more than thirty-year-old drama is instructive and memorable reading both for a generation too young to have lived through the assassination and for those who remember those days vividly but did not experience them from behind the scenes.

Stanley, Jerry. *Digger: The Tragic Fate of the California Indians from the Missions to the Gold Rush.* New York: Crown, 1997. (ISBN: 0-517-70951-1, trade / 0-517-70952-X, library). 103 pp. Ages 12 and up.

Digger is divided into three parts: California Indian life before white contact, the mission period of Spanish colonization, and the gold rush, when Americans from all walks of life overran the fledgling state. For native peoples of California, the period from the founding of the first Spanish mission to the height of the gold rush was one of great violence and destruction. While Spanish priests and soldiers desired to convert native peoples to Christianity, the experience of natives was one of hunger, disease, rebellion, and death. Many facts will be difficult for young audiences to understand and assimilate, just as the detailed truth of African American slavery unsettles.

Digger includes maps, a chronology, prints, and a glossary of selected California Indian tribal names, which makes it a valuable classroom resource. A recommended companion to *Digger* is *California's Indians and the Gold Rush* by Clifford E. Trafzer (Sierra Oaks, 1989), a Wyandot Indian historian, because of its depiction of California Indian response to profound social change. Teachers might want to refer to a newer book edited by Trafzer and Joel R. Hyer, *"Exterminate Them": Written Accounts of the Murder, Rape, and Slavery of Native Americans* (Michigan State University Press, 1999). In this book, the mythic image of rough-and-tumble miners who steadfastly worked along grand and rushing rivers is destroyed by original newspaper articles that describe the murder, rape, and enslavement of Native Americans.

Wick, Walter. *A Drop of Water: A Book of Science and Wonder.* Illustrated with photographs. New York: Scholastic, 1997. (ISBN: 0-590-22197-3). 40 pp. Ages 8 and up.

In this spectacular photo-essay, the reader witnesses all of water's amazing states: from ice and frost to steam, from dew to rainbow, from droplet to wave. Children will be amazed at Wick's recreation of science experiments from books written for children over 100 years ago. His photographic techniques date back to 1878. Detailed with each photo masterpiece is a short scientific essay about each water form and its transformations. *A Drop of Water* is simply written and filled with analogies children will understand: "When the surface of a drop of water shrinks to its smallest size, the drop forms a sphere. The sphere stretches because of the drop's weight and motion, but surface tension helps keep the drop together, as if it were held in an elastic skin" (p. 9). The full-color photographs lend the book elegance. Most impressive is an eight-inch snowflake, magnified sixty times its actual size.

A Drop of Water ends, like the old-fashioned science books, with a list of simple experiments that are sure to lure younger readers into the world of scientific investigation. With the simplest of tools, children will watch molecules in motion, surface tension at work, and more. *A Drop around the World* by Barbara Shaw McKinney (Dawn, 1998) would be a perfect accompaniment. This is an entertaining book about the water cycle, with flawless artwork and an engaging rhyme scheme.

1998 Orbis Pictus Recommended Titles

Collard III, Sneed B. *Animal Dads*. Illustrated by Steve Jenkins. Boston: Houghton Mifflin, 1997.

Cooper, Ilene. *The Dead Sea Scrolls*. Illustrated by John Thompson. New York: Morrow Junior Books, 1997.

Cox, Clinton. *Fiery Vision: The Life and Death of John Brown*. New York: Scholastic, 1997.

Fradin, Dennis Brindell. *The Planet Hunters: The Search for Other Worlds*. New York: McElderry/Simon & Schuster, 1997.

Gillette, J. Lynett. *Dinosaur Ghosts: The Mystery of Coelophysis*. Illustrated by Douglas Henderson. New York: Dial Books, 1997.

Ling, Mary, & Atkinson, Mary. *The Snake Book*. New York: Dorling Kindersley, 1997.

Lyons, Mary E. *Catching the Fire: Philip Simmons, Blacksmith*. Photographs by Mannie Garcia. Boston: Houghton Mifflin, 1997.

Mann, Elizabeth. *The Great Wall*. Illustrated by Alan Witschonke. New York: Mikaya, 1997.

Mochizuki, Ken. *Passage to Freedom: The Sugihara Story*. Illustrated by Dom Lee. New York: Lee & Low, 1997.

Pfeffer, Wendy. *A Log's Life*. Illustrated by Robin Brickman. New York: Simon & Schuster, 1997.

Simon, Seymour. *The Brain: Our Nervous System*. New York: Morrow Junior Books, 1997.

Tillage, Leon Walter. *Leon's Story*. Collage art by Susan L. Roth. New York: Farrar, Straus and Giroux, 1997.

**1999
Orbis Pictus
Award**

Armstrong, Jennifer. *Shipwreck at the Bottom of the World: The Extraordinary True Story of Shackleton and the* Endurance. New York: Crown, 1998. (ISBN: 0-517-80013-6, trade / 0-517-80014-4, library). 134 pp. Ages 10 and up.

First and foremost a survival story, Armstrong's account of Sir Ernest Shackleton's attempt to cross the Antarctic is a tightly woven account of the seemingly doomed but extraordinary *Endurance* adventure. Just a month and a half into the expedition, the *Endurance* and her crew are caught fast in the heavy pack of ice that surrounds the Antarctic. A series of disasters follows in which the ice tightens and the *Endurance* must be abandoned, as must a makeshift camp on ice. There are killer whales, hurricanes, melting ice floes, freak currents, and lost rudders to be overcome. Throughout it all, Shackleton leads, and his accomplishment—twenty-seven men held together and brought back alive—has become one of the greatest survival stories of all time.

Shipwreck exemplifies sound scholarship. Armstrong used the best books written on the subject, as well as Shackleton's own writing, and she traveled to the Scott Polar Research Institute in Cambridge, England, to examine precious logbooks and original photographs.

As a read-aloud, *Shipwreck* could be used for several purposes, from telling the incredible story of one man's ability to overcome fear and all personal considerations for the sake of others, to an exploration of how a writer captures and maintains an audience. As part of a unit on modern-day exploration, the book could be one of several, including *Ice Story: Shackleton's Lost Expedition* by Elizabeth Cody Kimmel (Clarion, 1999). Kimmel's delightful book is written as a detective story, well documented, and without fictional elements.

**1999
Orbis Pictus
Honor Books**

Burleigh, Robert. *Black Whiteness: Admiral Byrd Alone in the Antarctic.* Illustrated by Walter Lyon Krudop. New York: Atheneum, 1998. (ISBN: 0-689-81299-X). 36 pp. Ages 7 and up.

Burleigh introduces readers to Admiral Byrd's 1934 ordeal as he conducted scientific research in Antarctica. The research had two purposes: to learn about the continent—temperature, moisture, wind speed—and to explore what it is like to live completely alone, which he did for months in an underground structure. It is also a story about endurance and brilliance.

Byrd became gravely ill and had little hope of rescue. Through sheer cleverness, he thought to fly a kite, sending out a blazing beacon.

The general information for the text and illustrations was based on Admiral Byrd's own diary, *Alone* (International Collectors Library, 1938). Excerpts from *Alone,* reproduced in a cursive script, help students understand the deep connection between observation, science, and the precision that poetic language offers: "The tunnels are dark as dungeons. . . . Icicles on the roof glisten like candelabra; the walls glow with a sharp, blue nakedness" (p. 5).

The book would make a wonderful read-aloud and is a fine introduction to painting word pictures. During the reading aloud, students might draw pastel or chalk sketches before looking at Walter Krudop's captivating oil paintings. Older students who would like to know more about this unusual man will undoubtedly want to turn to *Alone.* Students interested in following the author's style might read *Flight: The Journey of Charles Lindbergh* (Philomel, 1991) and *Home Run: The Story of Babe Ruth* (Harcourt, 1998).

Holmes, Thom. *Fossil Feud: The Rivalry of the First American Dinosaur Hunters.* Illustrated by Thom Holmes. Parsippany, NJ: Messner, 1998. (ISBN: 0-382-39148-9). 160 pp. Ages 8 and up.

This carefully researched book is about two early, prominent paleontologists, Edward Drinker Cope and Othniel Charles Marsh, who added greatly to the world of science yet managed to display such bad character that one must ask, "Do the ends justify the means?" A feud between the two began because "Cope and Marsh were always out for themselves, always seeking a competitive advantage" (p. 14). This feud began when Marsh requested that a set of important new bones be sent to him at Yale University rather than to Cope at the Academy of Natural Sciences in Philadelphia. Neither ever got over the outcome of this struggle. Holmes brings the feud to riveting life with the help of his illustrator and the book's design artist. Readers will appreciate the fine and unusual interplay between type size, illustrations, and the designer's placement of drawings, photos, time lines, and lists.

This is a book as much about philosophy, economics, and journalism as it is about paleontology. For students interested in dinosaurs and/or the history of paleontology, the book offers rules for what makes a dinosaur a dinosaur, diagrams of basic anatomical features of a dinosaur, a geologic time line, a listing of the 335 genera of dinosaurs in the order in which they were discovered, a reading list, and a listing of North American dinosaur museums. For students interested in ethical issues, it is a gold mine of information on how means do or do not justify ends. The book might also accompany a study in financial planning; Marsh had deeper pockets than Cope and spent his money wisely. It could, finally, be read to explore the power of journalism, because of the multiple and far-reaching involvement of the press.

Jenkins, Steve. *Hottest, Coldest, Highest, Deepest.* Boston: Houghton Mifflin, 1998. (ISBN: 0-395-89999-0). 32 pp. Ages 8 and up.

This eye-catching introduction to geography brings the saying "all is relative" to life. The book does more than identify the earth's hottest, coldest, highest, and deepest places; it contextualizes the numbers associated with these wonders by carefully inserting maps (global and regional), measurement charts (often using humans and the Empire State Building for scale), and diagrams that help the reader visualize just *how* high, or just *how* deep. Clear print, combined with Jenkins's meticulously cut paper collages, contribute to the book's success.

While reading the book, children will feel the amazing natural world as they climb the highest mountain, dive into the deepest lake, navigate the longest river, and understand the most active volcano. For children who love hyperbole and prefer slight text with strong visuals, this is the perfect choice. Teachers can use *Hottest* along with Jenkins's many other books, including *Top of the World: Climbing Mount Everest* (Houghton Mifflin, 1999), in an author study.

Lobel, Alita. *No Pretty Pictures: A Child of War.* New York: Greenwillow Press, 1998. (ISBN: 0-688-15935-4). 193 pp. Ages 12 and up.

"I was born in Krakow, Poland. In the wrong place at the wrong time" (p. xi). So opens this gripping memoir of a child living "placidly with parents in a pleasant house with a living room" (p. xiii), a terrifying story told in the first person. When she was barely five years old, the Nazis came to Lobel's town. Because they were Jewish, she and her little brother spent the next five years in hiding and on the run. Eventually they were captured and transported to three different concentration camps. Sick with lice, diarrhea, and tuberculosis, both were rescued, sent to Sweden, and finally reunited with their parents. The child's viewpoint is the strength of this book. The narrator never sermonizes or presents herself as a victim; instead, she tells the story clearly using a prose style based on detail:

> We went inside one of the barracks. Away from the icy air, from the blinding glare of the searchlights, from the shoving and the shouting, from the woman who had tried too late to barter my brother for her son, from the burst of the rifle shots, I tried to speak. Where is my brother going? . . . Somewhere behind my chattering teeth, my tongue was a dead fish, stuck, glued, useless. (p. 88–89)

No one would expect an illustrator of children's books to have had such experiences. The wise classroom teacher will bring in additional books by Lobel such as *On Market Street* (Scholastic, 1982) and *Toads and Diamonds* (Greenwillow, 1966). Because this survivor still believes "my life has been good" (p. 190), discussions about survivors, whether explorer or victim, might illuminate the qualities of those who experience living hell yet risk again, or somehow learn to forgive.

1999 Orbis Pictus Recommended Titles

Bateman, Robert. *Safari.* Boston: Little, Brown, 1998.

Blumberg, Rhoda. *What's the Deal? Jefferson, Napoleon, and the Louisiana Purchase.* Washington, DC: National Geographic Society, 1998.

Fradin, Dennis. *Samuel Adams: The Father of American Independence.* New York: Clarion Books, 1998.

Freedman, Russell. *Martha Graham: A Dancer's Life.* New York: Clarion Books, 1998

Lowry, Lois. *Looking Back: A Book of Memories.* Boston: Houghton Mifflin, 1998.

Martin, Jacqueline Briggs. *Snowflake Bentley.* Illustrated by Mary Azarian. Boston: Houghton Mifflin, 1998.

Matthews, Tom L. *Light Shining through the Mist: A Photobiography of Dian Fossey.* Washington, DC: National Geographic Society, 1998.

Partridge, Elizabeth. *Restless Spirit: The Life and Work of Dorothea Lange.* New York: Viking, 1998.

Pinkney, Andrea Davis. *Duke Ellington.* Illustrated by Brian Pinkney. New York: Hyperion, 1998.

Reinhard, Johan. *Discovering the Inca Ice Maiden: My Adventures on Ampato.* Washington, DC: National Geographic Society, 1998.

Stalcup, Ann. *On the Home Front: Growing Up in Wartime England.* North Haven, CT: Linnet/ Shoe String Press, 1998.

Stanley, Diane. *Joan of Arc.* New York: Morrow Junior Books, 1998.

Stanley, Jerry. *Frontier Merchants: Lionel and Barron Jacobs and the Jewish Pioneers Who Settled the West.* New York: Crown, 1998.

Thomas, Jane Resh. *Behind the Mask: The Life of Queen Elizabeth I.* New York: Clarion Books, 1998.

Warren, Andrea. *Pioneer Girl: Growing Up on the Prairie.* New York: Morrow Junior Books, 1998.

Section III Appendix

**2000
Orbis Pictus
Award**

Bridges, Ruby. *Through My Eyes.* Illustrated with photographs. New York: Scholastic, 1999. (ISBN: 0-590-18923-9). 64 pp. Ages 8 and up.

"When I was six years old, the civil rights movement came knocking at the door. It was 1960, and history pushed in and swept me up in a whirlwind" (p. 4). So begins the emotion-packed story of Ruby Bridges, the one black child sent to integrate the William Franz elementary school in New Orleans. Each day, she walked resolutely past an angry crowd of parents, teenagers, and children who were infuriated by her presence in *their* school. These people and others—including the governor of Louisiana—vowed never to comply with the federal court's deadline for school integration. This is the story of how—despite these conditions— Ruby's courage, strength, and stamina won out over injustice, bigotry, and prejudice, so that, by the end of the year, white children began to return to the Franz school and integration was accomplished. The story is unusually compelling because the focus of this historical turnaround was a six-year-old named Ruby Bridges.

Readers familiar with *The Story of Ruby Bridges* (Scholastic, 1995) by child psychiatrist Robert Coles will notice the additional content offered in this account. The now-adult Ruby Bridges provides a unique perspective by telling readers what she understood and felt about the situation *then* as a six-year-old, and what she understands and feels *now* as an adult. This then-and-now account is further enriched by numerous photographs; excerpts from newspapers, magazines, and books; and quotes from John Steinbeck, Robert Coles, Ruby's first-grade teacher, and Ruby's mother. This supportive material adds depth to the already engaging words of Ruby Bridges and allows readers the opportunity to pull together the different voices telling the story.

No discussion of this book would be complete without mentioning the inspiring presence of Ruby's teacher, Barbara

The appendix is a reprint, with minor revisions, of the Talking about Books section in *Language Arts 78* (November 2000), pp. 177–84.

Henry. Shunned by both her principal and her fellow teachers, she welcomed Ruby as the sole student in her class and in time grew to love and admire her. At the end of this gripping historical narrative, Ruby Bridges brings us up to date on her life, telling us about her reunion with Mrs. Henry and Dr. Coles, and her more recent work in inner-city public schools, including the Franz school where this story first began. This inspiring story brings issues of equality, fairness, and justice vividly to life. It shows how the brave actions of a single child can make a difference. (MZ)

2000 Orbis Pictus Honor Books

Myers, Walter Dean. *At Her Majesty's Request: An African Princess in Victorian England.* New York: Scholastic, 1999. (ISBN: 0-590-48669-1). 146 pp. Ages 11 and up.

In a rare bookshop in London, Walter Dean Myers discovered a packet of letters detailing the life of Sarah Forbes Bonetta, an African princess rescued from certain death as part of a ritual sacrifice in West Africa and brought to England by a compassionate Commander Forbes. In *At Her Majesty's Request: An African Princess in Victorian England,* Myers has done an admirable job telling Sarah's story.

The design of the book is unique. Done in sepia tones and illustrated with prints of the time, Myers's consistent choice of brown on white seems to be a commentary about the conflicting life a black child would have within a wealthy, white, nineteenth-century environment. There is a sense of isolation here, a serenity, but one that lacks possibilities—in this case, color.

Sarah is well treated in England. She is under the protection of Queen Victoria and as such, enjoys a unique position. Nonetheless, she remains a curiosity. We learn that she entered into a loveless marriage with James Davies, a successful black businessman—a marriage encouraged by the Queen. "What did Sarah feel? She was marrying a man she felt she could never truly love. But Mrs. Schoen had consoled her, and the royal family had made the wedding seem right" (p. 118). After her husband's business fails, Sarah returns to Africa, settling in Lagos. In 1880, she traveled to Madeira to recover from illness in its healthful climate. While there, her short and only sporadically happy life came to an end.

Myers's story is a compelling one, which is sure to hold the attention of young readers. It showcases the merger of fine research with gifted storytelling, a hallmark of Walter Dean Myers's work. (KPS)

Reich, Susanna. *Clara Schumann: Piano Virtuoso.* New York: Clarion Books, 1999. (ISBN: 0-395-89119-1). 118 pp. Ages 11 and up.

In 1844, all of Moscow was in a buzz. A marvelous piano virtuoso had come to the city. Her talent was beyond that which had ever been seen before. Susanna Reich's *Clara Schumann: Piano Virtuoso* is the bittersweet story of the nineteenth century's most famous female pianist. In clear, informative language, Reich presents a portrait of a woman who, while famous in her time, has not received nearly enough recognition in the present day. Now eclipsed by her famous contemporaries, husband Robert Schumann and beloved friend Johannes Brahms, Clara Schumann was a woman well ahead of her time. Reich recounts her difficult yet inspiring childhood that was ruled and determined by her forceful and enterprising father, whose main priority was to achieve fame and glory through his young daughter. Yet Schumann emerges as a strong woman.

Reich offers a well-balanced look at this quintessential widowed mother of seven—a mother who works an almost impossible schedule, playing concerts around Europe to earn money to support her children. Reich is not over-idealistic in her portrayal. The audience comes to understand that Schumann was an ambitious woman who, while totally devoted to her children, craved audience applause. Reproductions of portraits of Schumann, as well as photographs taken late in her life toward the end of the nineteenth century, support an image of a woman who was self-assured in her musical ability yet immersed in the shadow of an unhappy life.

In Reich's final chapter, entitled "Pieces of a Puzzle," she discusses aspects of her research and the types of documents, letters, and diaries she drew upon for this book. This is an important tool for young readers, offering them a glimpse of what it takes to research and write about historical personages. During a time when music history seems to be a little-known area for children and to many adults, Reich reminds us of what we are missing by not learning more about the great musicians of the past. (KPS)

Johnson, Sylvia. *Mapping the World.* New York: Atheneum, 1999.
(ISBN: 0-689-81813-0). 32 pp. Ages 9 and up.

Claudius Ptolemaus, Matthew Paris, Martin Waldseemuller,
and Gerardus Mercator had a common interest—cartography—an interest in mapping the world. In Sylvia Johnson's
book *Mapping the World,* a reader can trace the history of
mapmaking from an early Babylonian clay-tablet carving, to a
Mercator projection from the 1500s, to maps generated
through satellites' remote-sensing and computer technology.

In this clearly organized volume, the color reproductions of
ancient, medieval, exploration-age, and modern-age maps
complement Johnson's lucid prose. The list of additional
readings presents books that will be of particular interest to
upper elementary school and middle school students. While
cartography once was a skill few could master, the geography
information system (GIS) provides everyone with the tools to
create technically accurate and sophisticated maps. Johnson's
brief introduction to this computer-generated mapmaking tool
is enough to entice children to try their hands at an ancient art.
Teachers can expand students' awareness of maps and their
two-dimensional representation of three-dimensional space by
sharing *Atlas in the Round* (Running Press, 1999). *Ultimate
Panoramic Atlas* (Dorling Kindersley, 1998) and *World Atlas for
Young Explorers* (National Geographic, 1998) will provide other
views of this fascinating human endeavor and the physical
and cultural landscape. (RMK)

Montgomery, Sy. *The Snake Scientist.* Illustrated with photographs
by Nic Bishop. New York: Houghton Mifflin, 1999.
(ISBN: 0-395-87169-7). 48 pp. Ages 9 and up.

Bob Mason is enthralled with the yearly gifts he receives—
sacks full of snakes. Each spring, people from all parts of the
world come to Manitoba, Canada, to assist this Oregon State
University zoologist in his study of red-sided garter snakes. In
The Snake Scientist, we experience the scientific process in
action. For fifteen years, Mason has been observing and ex-
perimenting with these snakes. In this book, a volume in the
Scientists in the Field series, Mason hypothesizes that garters
use trails of pheromones, chemicals given off by the reptile
that influence their behavior in migrating to feeding grounds,
tracking down potential mates, and locating their own dens.

Through controlled experiments and field observations, we see Mason unravel reptilian mysteries of the natural world.

Through color photography of the snakes and those handling them, and through a lucid text, children will learn about snakes as the process of science unfolds. This book could be used with Bianca Lavies' *A Gathering of Garter Snakes* (Dutton, 1993) to expand children's awareness of scientific fieldwork. *The Snake Scientist* makes information accessible through the inclusion of an index, a map of the Narcisse Snake Dens, a booklist for further reading, and an Internet resource. Finally, in the spirit of the scientific process, the book concludes with a list of questions that Mason and his team have raised and intend to explore. (RMK)

Jenkins, Steve. *The Top of the World.* New York: Houghton Mifflin, 1999. (ISBN: 0-395-94218-7). Unpaged. Ages 8 and up.

In *The Top of the World*, Steve Jenkins takes the reader to Nepal and the intrigue of the world's highest mountain, Everest. Jenkins incorporates information on climate, geography, geology, altitude, history, medical concerns, ecological issues, climbing gear, and history as he pushes readers to the 29,000-foot summit. This outstanding picture book is an invitation to learn more about Mt. Everest, the people who love and respect it, as well as those who intrude on its majesty.

The author-illustrator's paper-collage illustrations are extraordinary. Skillfully coordinated with the text, crushed and cut papers carve the beauty and danger of the mountain and the human challengers. Jenkins uses sidebars and labels throughout to add interesting, supportive, and sometimes necessary information without distracting readers from the main focus. His collages provide clarity, focus, and tactile appreciation of the subject more effectively than photographs could have.

Young readers may receive lessons in planning, dedication, and goal setting while participating in this literary trek. In addition, they may be motivated to learn more about this world treasure. Jenkins provides for this interest. On the final page, the author presents a bibliography of books and Web sites for further investigation as well as an impressive list of Mt. Everest records for those who savor such particulars. (CD)

Other Outstanding Nonfiction Titles

Views from the Artistic World

Macaulay, David. *Building the Book* Cathedral. New York: Houghton Mifflin, 1999. (ISBN: 0-395-92147-3). 112 pp. Ages 11 and up.

In contemporary society, process is often sacrificed at the expense of product. David Macaulay is an architect who has always had a reverence for sharing with a relatively young audience the way things are done artistically. In 1973, Macaulay introduced his process approach to young readers in his first book *Cathedral,* which details the building of a French Gothic cathedral dating from the thirteenth century. In his most recent book, *Building the Book* Cathedral, the artist takes us back in time to the creation of his now famous work.

Written in first person, Macaulay's book brings the evolution of his concept closer to the reader. He is a self-acknowledged, lifelong learner. Like its predecessor, *Building the Book* Cathedral is a large-format work, well suited to the grand scale of the subject. His drawings are accompanied by succinct yet informative text, explaining the inspiration and reasons for certain artistic decisions.

At times, large, dark drawings are juxtaposed with finely detailed renderings, offering a broad look at this artist's talent. A cavernous, dark image of the outside of the cathedral is, for example, followed by pages from his sketchbooks, offering different penciled perspectives of the building. On the page following, however, we see the finished product that incorporates the sketchbook views, only now the images are clear, detailed, and executed with a sense of finality.

Macaulay reiterates his original text and in smaller print, comments on it. This functions, in effect, as a content footnote that can be read and enjoyed without interfering with the narration. Macaulay reflects on and reconsiders his earlier text, inviting the audience to do the same. But the reader is left wishing he had included different drafts of the text so the path to the final concept could be traced. Nonetheless, *Building the Book* Cathedral serves as a valuable revisiting of a groundbreaking work. (KPS)

Micklethwait, Lucy. *A Child's Book of Art: Discover Great Paintings.* New York: Dorling Kindersley, 1999. (ISBN: 0-7894-4283-3). 32 pp. Ages 8 and up.

Children of all ages who are unable or who have been unwilling to spend time with graphic art masterpieces are the beneficiaries of this Lucy Micklethwait book. She has selected thirteen paintings reflecting several periods, topics, painters, and styles as the solid foundation of *A Child's Book of Art*. Her focus is clearly stated in her introductory page entitled "How to Investigate a Painting," which begins, "A painting is like an unsolved mystery" (p. 3). The approach is fresh and appealing to beginners in art appreciation.

The layout of this oversized book is consistent. It includes the painting and title, an investigation section, detailed notations, size comparisons, and biographical information on the artist. The investigation sections, in which she isolates objects from the painting, are a dynamic part of her effort to tease the reader into engaging with the painting. Besides the objects, the reader might find questions like those on the page with Valazquez's "An Old Woman Cooking Eggs": "What might this boy be thinking? What would the woman use this for? If you could touch this pitcher, how would it feel?" (p. 12).

Purists may be critical of this simplistic attempt to encourage appreciation. Yet those who wonder what art lovers are doing when they stare for long periods of time at a painting will find that *A Child's Book of Art* sets them on a path toward understanding. For the many children who will never visit an art museum, this book may be their only guided tour; for others it will be an invitation. (CD)

Aliki. *William Shakespeare & the Globe*. New York: HarperCollins, 1999. (ISBN: 0-06-027820-X, trade / 0-06-027821-8, library). 48 pp. Ages 10 and up.

Introduced by quotations from Shakespearean works, Aliki's newest book offers graphic and verbal pictures of Shakespeare himself, theater conditions of his times, and the rebuilding of the Globe Theatre in modern London. Written as a five-act drama in much the same style as were Shakespeare's own plays, this colorful book includes information about the milieu of London and the growth of theatres, dropping names like Elizabeth I, James Burbage, and Christopher Marlowe, all important influences on Shakespeare's own success. Captions under whimsical drawings of Shakespeare's characters, his environment, and his peers add exciting facts that help illuminate the period. Readers will recognize famous lines from many of Shakespeare's works and be intrigued to read more from his creations as well as learn more about Elizabethan dramatic times. The chronological list of plays and poems, words and expressions created by Shakespeare, and places to visit today in Shakespeare's old stomping grounds are helpful for novice students of Shakespeare and his works. An entire act is devoted to Sam Wanamaker who led the 1997 rebuilding of a modern replica of the Globe, helping first-time readers of Shakespeare to leap from the 1600s to today. This unique approach to a difficult subject for younger readers makes Shakespeare's contributions accessible to even the most timid reader. (CL)

Curlee, Lynn. *Rushmore.* New York: Scholastic, 1999. (ISBN: 0-590-22573-1). 48 pp. Ages 10 and up.

This book chronicles one man's quest to leave a visual reminder of "men whose achievements represent the founding, expansion, preservation and conservation of America" (p. 8). Gutzon Borglum, sculptor and engineer, called the stone carving on Mount Rushmore "The Shrine of Democracy." But from the start, controversy surrounded the project. While many agreed that Washington, Jefferson, and Lincoln should be included in this monument, Theodore Roosevelt was a controversial choice. Some felt the recently deceased Woodrow Wilson should be enshrined on Mount Rushmore. After all, he had led the United States through the First World War. Others formed a grassroots campaign, arguing that the champion of equality for women, Susan B. Anthony, should be the fourth figure. But, even though federal money would finance the project, Borglum stood his ground and moved forward with his work and his choices.

This book details the many obstacles that Borglum had to overcome, including financial difficulty during and beyond the Great Depression and technical problems in sculpting such enormous figures. Borglum's original intent to carve the four men to the waist was abandoned upon his death and Borglum's son, Lincoln, finished the work on the faces. *Rushmore* provides a visual and textual tribute to one of America's dreamers, an accomplished artist, Gutzon Borglum. Curlee's acrylic paintings capture the grandeur of Borglum's work. A map of South Dakota at the beginning of the book will help children locate Mount Rushmore on the American landscape. A time line at the end gives an overview of the chronology of the sculpting process. (RMK)

Hamanaka, Sheila, & Ohmi, Ayano. *In Search of the Spirit: The Living National Treasures of Japan.* Photographs by Sheila Hamanaka. New York: Morrow Junior Books, 1999. (ISBN: 0-688-14607-4, trade / 0-688-14608-2, library) 48 pp. Ages 10 and up.

Fabric dying, basket weaving, puppet making, sword making, acting, and ceramic sculpting—what is unique about this set of crafts? These ancient arts were developed in sixteenth-century Japan and have been preserved through dedicated artisans who passed on their sometimes secret skills from generation to generation. During World War II, these art forms began to disappear. In order to keep the old traditions alive, the Japanese government decided to honor the traditional craftmasters who had sacrificed and devoted their lives to their art. These traditional craftspersons and performing artists were provided grants to support their lifelong work and to train apprentices. Since the 1950s, over 100 men and women have been given the title of "Bearers of Important Intangible Cultural Assets"—or appropriately, "Living National Treasures."

In this presentation, Sheila Hamanaka and Ayano Ohmi have taken young readers into the personal working lives of six extraordinary artists. Each chapter is highlighted with beautiful photographs of the honored Living National Treasure engaging in representative works of her or his craft. Hamanaka also has illustrated each section with step-by-step outlines of a particular aspect of each artist's creation. Just as the Living National Treasures "are passing on something intangible—the spirit of Japan's ancient culture," so Hamanaka and Ohmi are sharing these honored individuals and their crafts with young readers. (EA)

Views from the Scientific World

Sill, Cathryn. *About Reptiles: A Guide for Children.* Illustrated by John Sill. Atlanta, GA: Peachtree, 1999. (ISBN: 1-56145-183-5). Unpaged. Ages 5–9.

> Reptiles have dry, scaly skin.
> Some reptiles have a hard, bony plate.
> Reptiles have short legs . . .
> Or no legs at all. (unpaged)

These are the opening pages of *About Reptiles*, a nonfiction science book for the early reader. Each page boldly presents the young scientist with a fact. Each facing page supports the information with a beautifully detailed illustration of the unique reptile in its most common habitat or environment. The collaboration between Cathryn Sill, an elementary teacher, and her husband, a wildlife artist, truly supports the young observer's ability to read a beginning science text. For example, facing the bold print, "Reptiles have short legs" (unpaged) is a fully illustrated color plate of a Texas horned lizard. Turning the page, the words, "or no legs at all" (unpaged) focus readers on a slender glass lizard, that looks like a snake. The juxtaposition helps young readers to recognize the contrast between these two reptiles.

Assisting interested adult or child readers, the final pages of the book include an afterword that reprints the full-color plates in black and white and provides more detailed information about each reptile. It is here that we learn that the slender glass lizards "get their name from their tail which, when grabbed, will shatter into several pieces. They live in dry grasslands and dry, open woods" (unpaged). This is a simple book on reptiles, an example of a science book for the emergent reader. (EA)

Norell, Mark A., & Dingus, Lowell. *A Nest of Dinosaurs: The Story of Oviraptor.* New York: Doubleday Book for Young Readers, 1999. (ISBN: 0-385-32558-4). 42 pp. Ages 11 and up.

From its eye-catching red cover to the science-in-discovery photographs and lifelike drawings of oviraptorid dinosaurs, Norell and Dingus cycle readers through the scientific process of discovery. Their unearthing of 72-million-year-old dinosaur skeleton parts in the Mongolian Gobi Desert surprised even professional paleontologists. From fieldwork to museum analysis, the authors extrapolate from tiny eggshell fragments and paint a picture of the living conditions of dinosaurs, and prove that they sat on nests of eggs. The fossil findings suggest that the oviraptorid, meat-eating dinosaurs were protective parents who nurtured their offspring, a discovery that changed everything they had believed about these Cretaceous period creatures. Norell and Dingus concluded that dinosaurs are not extinct; birds are today's living dinosaurs, linked by their flexible hand joints and the brooding of eggs.

Like real scientific detectives, Norell and Dingus also explain what cannot be extrapolated from the findings. They leave many questions unanswered about oviraptorids. Sand-colored sidebars explain how scientific theories are developed and add personal details about this discovery and about paleontology in general. The authors' voices give an immediacy to the discoveries that make us want to venture to the Ukhaa Tolgod exploration site, searching for our own sand-and-mud-covered bird ancestors. The thrill of changing scientific beliefs about the evolution of modern day birds will satisfy the cravings of even fifth-grade dinosaur fans. Dingus, Chiappe, and Chiappe's *The Tiniest Giants* (Doubleday, 1999) could be used to satisfy any eager young scientist's search for additional information on the topic. (CL)

Views from the Historic World

Donoughue, Carol. *The Mystery of the Hieroglyphs: The Story of the Rosetta Stone and the Race to Decipher Egyptian Hieroglyphs.* New York: Oxford University Press, 1999. (ISBN: 0-19-521554-0, trade/ 0-19-521553-2, library). 48 pp. Ages 9 and up.

This narrative, with the purposeful use of the word *mystery* in its title, depicts the story of the 1799 discovery of the Rosetta Stone and the race to decipher Egyptian hieroglyphs. Once deciphered, scholars could read the writing covering the statues, temples, and mummy cases that have been found among the ruins of ancient Egypt. As with all good mysteries, the details of unfolding events are revealed step-by-step: the discovery of the Rosetta Stone by the French, its appropriation by the British, and the steps leading to its deciphering. The chapters on decoding the stone highlight the work of Thomas Young and Jean François Champollion and serve as a profound example of scholarship building upon itself, ultimately leading to illumination and insight. The text is lively and thorough. Donoughue clarifies difficult points with many photographs, drawings, maps, a time line, a glossary, and an index.

Young readers will delight in a whole chapter devoted to basic information on how to read hieroglyphs, and in the interactive exercises throughout the book, which get them working as Young and Champollion might have. They will come to under-stand the important role of cartouches in unlocking the mys-tery of the Rosetta Stone, learn facts about how Egyptians wrote (in all directions, often wrapped around pictures), and gain insight into Egyptian culture. Students will certainly appreciate the discussion of how young boys became scribes, which was considered to be very important, and will most likely squirm as they read: "A boy's ears are on his back; he listens when he is beaten" (p. 11). (RN)

Haskins, James, & Benson, Kathleen. *Bound for America: The Forced Migration of Africans to the New World.* Paintings by Floyd

Cooper. New York: Lothrop, Lee & Shepard, 1999.
(ISBN: 0-688-10258-1, trade / 0-688-10529-X, library). 48 pp.
Ages 10 and up.

Haskins and Benson describe the horrors of dealing in human beings, from earliest civilizations to the economic slave trade between European countries and the New World. Floyd Cooper's oil wash illustrations show the dignity and individuality of African tribes. Photographs and paintings help readers envision the fate of slaves. Separate sections describe the abominations of slavery, from forcefully taking people from their homes, to brandings and force-feedings, to inhumane conditions on "slavers" where people committed suicide and mutinied in defiance of their captors, to diseases waiting to decimate them. Taking almost half the book, the authors describe the Middle Passage, shipping routes between Africa and the New World, including accounts of slaves forced to dance for exercise and others mutilated and hung or thrown overboard for attempted mutinies. The one successful mutiny of slaves from Sierra Leone on board the *Amistad* adds little relief. Milestones in the history of slavery involving Africans demonstrate the expanse of slavery's time frame from 1441 to 1808. A bibliography and an index augment the usefulness of this book. Seeing the jet-black cover with an African man in neck rings, readers will approach this book with an impending sense of man's inhumanity to man. For a lighter approach to the same topic, see Walter Dean Myers's *At Her Majesty's Request* (Scholastic, 1999), or for an additional perspective, see Julius Lester's *From Slave Ship to Freedom Road* (Dial Books for Young Readers, 1998). (CL)

Bartoletti, Susan Campbell. *Kids on Strike!* Illustrated with photographs. New York: Houghton Mifflin, 1999. (ISBN: 0-395-88892-1). 208 pp. Ages 10 and up.

Child labor was commonplace in the United States in the mid-1800s and early 1900s. Instead of going to school, kids worked in mills, glass houses, coal mines, and on the city streets as messengers, newsies, and bootblacks. They worked fourteen-hour days, in unsafe conditions, for low pay. But as Susan Campbell Bartoletti tells us, they did not quietly and complacently accept these conditions. Again and again, children protested for higher wages, safer conditions, and shorter hours. They were anything but passive.

Each chapter in this book is a vivid example of how kids pushed for better working conditions through that most dangerous but powerful of bargaining tools: a strike. Harriet Hanson, an 11-year-old mill worker in Lowell, Massachusetts, and her fellow spinners joined a strike coordinated by the Factory Girls' Association. They were protesting the dangerous machines, noise, lint, unventilated rooms, long hours, and poor wages. Messenger boys in New York City protested the exorbitant fees they were charged for their uniforms and the company policy of paying only for telegrams accepted by recipients. Newsies who sold newspapers on the streets protested unfair price increases and the policy of not refunding the price of unsold newspapers. The children's efforts did make a difference. These stories show that "kids only wanted what adults wanted: a fair day's work, a fair day's wage, a safe working environment, and better living conditions" (p. 193). Kids who went on strike helped make it happen. (MZ)

Trailblazers: Outstanding Human Achievement

Severance, John B. *Einstein: Visionary Scientist.* Illustrated with photographs. New York: Clarion Books, 1999. (ISBN: 0-395-93100-2). 144 pp. Ages 10 and up.

Say the word *genius* and the name Albert Einstein (1879–1955) likely pops into your mind. But this father of modern physics, who challenged existing beliefs about how the universe works, is no example of the self-fulfilling prophecy. Born with a large, square-shaped head, Einstein was slow to speak, threw temper tantrums, and was labeled "mildly retarded." His school years were equally unpromising. According to his elementary school principal, "It didn't matter what profession the boy prepared for because he would never be successful at anything" (p. 17). Neither was he a favorite of teachers, who described him as lazy, dreamy, arrogant, averse to studying subjects that didn't interest him, and unwilling to let anyone tell him anything.

Einstein explained himself simply: "I live, I feel puzzled, and all the time I try to understand" (p. 123). Severance helps readers to understand Einstein's brilliance, eccentricity, and contradictions in a balanced, chronological portrait. We are reminded of influential scientists dating to Galileo; we learn about contemporaries such as Marie Curie; we follow the rise of an academic career in Europe and a 1933 arrival at Princeton University after fleeing the Nazis. Finally, from televisions, automatic garage door openers, grocery store scanners, compact disks, lasers, and other developments, we realize how Einstein's work—in this case a paper published in 1905 on the behavior of light—is shaping the present and future.

Severance explains both the complex science and a complex man using everyday contemporary examples, dozens of complementary black-and-white archival photographs, and end matter that includes a detailed chronology, a bibliography, and an index. Earlier subjects of Severance biographies include Churchill, Ghandi, and Jefferson. (J J)

Freedman, Russell. *Babe Didrikson Zaharias: The Making of a Champion.* Illustrated with photographs. New York: Clarion Books, 1999. (ISBN: 0-395-63367-2). 192 pp. Ages 10 and up.

Leave it to Russell Freedman to start with a sports figure and end up with a powerful human-interest story. Mildred Ella Didriksen (1911–1956), also known as Babe Didrikson (school records spelled her Norwegian birthname incorrectly, with her approval). Zaharias, the stage name of her professional wrestler husband, was a tomboy whose huge Texas ego was fed by the limelight. And there's no surprise in that because Babe— "she's a regular Babe Ruth" (p. 15)—was arguably the greatest athlete of the twentieth century. She could have bragged, "Okay, Babe's here. Now who's gonna finish second?" (p. 135) at the start of almost any athletic competition—track and field, volleyball, roller skating, tennis, golf, swimming, diving, baseball, basketball, billiards, or bowling. When a reporter asked, "Is there anything you don't play?", Babe responded, "Dolls" (p. 9). When questioned about her best sport, she answered, "I do everything best" (p. 77).

In a lifelong quest to be the greatest athlete that ever lived, Babe challenged prevailing norms related not only to athletic achievement but also to gender, social class, and public behavior. Indeed, readers need not like sports to like this book. Freedman transcends sports, capturing the times along with the relentless, self-confident, fiercely competitive spirit underlying Babe's athletic victories. In a concluding author's note, Freedman reflects on his subject as "a far more complex, contradictory, courageous, and endearing character than I imagined" (p. 166).

In *Lincoln* (Clarion, 1987), *The Wright Brothers* (Holiday House, 1991), *Eleanor Roosevelt* (Clarion, 1993), *Martha Graham* (Clarion, 1998), and other biographies, Russell Freedman has brought notable figures to life. With his trademark style— memorable quotations, revealing anecdotes, abundant black-and-white photographs, and engaging writing—he also has breathed life into Babe (p. 15). (JJ)

Beil, Karen Magnuson. *Fire in Their Eyes: Wildfires and the People Who Fight Them.* Illustrated with photographs. San Diego: Harcourt Brace, 1999. (ISBN: 0-15-201043-2, hardcover/ 0-15-201042-4, paper). 64 pp. Ages 9 and up.

With the opening chapter titled "Trapped," the reader wonders why anyone would want to be a firefighter. In just one second, human skin blisters and burns, eyelashes disintegrate, and hair turns to ash. "After four seconds the blistered skin chars and clothing bursts into flame. Then the fire arrives" (p. 7). In this informative examination of fires and firefighting and fire starting, Beil's narrative profiles a handful of men and women, capturing the danger, excitement, and drama of their lives. Beil's own photos of men and women working in the midst of fires, some raging out of control, vividly illustrate the tasks of all types of fighters: initial-attack teams, hotshot crews, smokejumpers, and prescribed-burn crews.

Following an extraordinary discussion of the rigorous training smokejumpers must go through, the book is organized by fire type, where the work of individual fighters is often profiled in depth. The Morrell Mountain travesty, for example, brings us close to Ron Marks, a smokejumper. Another chapter depicts the fire in Old Topanga Canyon, a community threatened by flame.

The book ends with a compelling discussion of the growing danger zone humans create as housing projects poke into wilderness areas. Beil also takes the opportunity to point out the huge role Native Americans play in developing policies for planned burns and the relationship of this role to Native American cultures. There is a glossary of terms, but no index. *Fire* (Clarion, 1998) by Dorothy Hinshaw Patent, which explains the science of forest fires and the controlled burn, is a fine companion piece. (RN)

Tallchief, Maria, with Wells, Rosemary. Illustrated by Gary Kelley. *Tallchief: America's Prima Ballerina.* New York: Viking, 1999. (ISBN: 0-670-88756-0). 28 pp. Ages 4–9.

Maria Tallchief collaborates with Rosemary Wells in *Maria Tallchief: America's Prima Ballerina,* sharing this Native American's story from ages three to seventeen. In the prologue, Wells explains her engagement with Maria Tallchief's story, and soon the reader too is engaged. We learn how music and dance shaped Tallchief and led her to become "prima ballerina." Gary Kelley's pastels and artistic vision connect with Maria's story and the softness of his graphics seizes the reader. Each two-page spread includes text and a focused pastel with an opposing full-page illustration. Three times in the 28-page book this text-illustration pattern is interrupted with a stirring two-page illustration without text that allows the reader to pause at a significant place in the story.

With her family's support, Tallchief overcame the cultural disdain of her Osage people and developed an extraordinary gift of music and movement. The first-person narrative has poetic overtones that blend fact with subjective expression. "I chose dance because I felt the music I loved grew inside of me in a different way than could be expressed by my hands on an instrument. It coursed through my body" (p. 16). For young readers who love ballet and even for those who do not, this story of passion, dedication, and talent has relevance. (CD)

A Final Note

To begin the second decade of the committee's work, we were pleased to see a number of books that focused on the geographic landscape and its representation in maps as well as on finely crafted biographical and autobiographical works for a wide range of readers. We also noted the appearance of numerous books dealing with dinosaurs and other wildlife that enable children to understand the scientific process and the dynamic nature of knowledge.

Elaine Aoki is Lower School Director at the Bush School, Seattle, Washington.

Christine Duthie is a first-grade teacher at Trumansburg Central School in Interlocken, New York.

Julie Jensen is Professor Emerita at the University of Texas at Austin.

Richard M. Kerper is Associate Professor of Elementary and Early Childhood Education at Millersville University in Millersville, Pennsylvania.

Carolyn Lott is Associate Professor of Curriculum and Instruction at the University of Montana in Missoula, Montana.

Ruth Nathan is a third-grade teacher at Rancho Romero School in Alamo, California.

Karen Patricia Smith is Professor of Library and Information Studies at Queens College in Flushing, New York.

Myra Zarnowski is Professor of Elementary and Early Childhood Education at Queens College in Flushing, New York.

Editors

Julie M. Jensen is professor emerita at The University of Texas at Austin. She is a graduate of the University of Minnesota and a former teacher in the Minneapolis public schools. Long active in the National Council of Teachers of English and its affiliates, Jensen was president of NCTE (1988) and winner of its Distinguished Service Award (1997). She has served NCTE's publication program as a member of the Editorial Board, as well as editor of *Language Arts* (1976–1983) and several NCTE book titles.

Richard M. Kerper is associate professor of children's literature and literacy in the Department of Elementary and Early Childhood Education at Millersville University in Pennsylvania. His research interests are nonfiction literature, visual literacy, and reader-based and text-based response to literature. These interests developed during the fifteen years he spent in elementary, middle, and high school classrooms in New Hampshire and during his doctoral studies at Ohio State University. His writing about nonfiction literature and visual literacy has appeared in *Making Facts Come Alive: Choosing Quality Nonfiction Literature K–8* (1998), *Young Adults and Public Libraries: A Handbook of Materials and Services* (1998), and the *Handbook of Research on Teaching Literacy through the Communicative and Visual Arts* (1997). Interviews he conducted with Jim Murphy and Jennifer Armstrong have appeared in *The New Advocate.* In addition, he has contributed reviews of nonfiction books appearing in *Language Arts* and *Childhood Education.*

Myra Zarnowski is professor in the School of Education at Queens College of the City University of New York, where she teaches courses on children's literature, literacy, and social studies. As a past chair and long-term member of the Orbis Pictus Award Committee, she got to indulge her passion for nonfiction by reading hundreds of books each year and sharing them with her students. This passion is reflected in her publications, including *Learning about Biographies: A Reading-and-Writing Approach for Children* (1990), *Children's Literature and Social Studies: Selecting and*

Using Notable Books in the Classroom (1993, co-edited with Arlene F. Gallagher), and articles in *The New Advocate, School Library Journal, The Reading Teacher,* and *CBC Forum.* She enjoys working with New York City teachers to incorporate nonfiction literature into their language arts and social studies programs.

Contributing Committee Members

Elaine M. Aoki received her Ph.D. from the University of Washington. She is currently an elementary principal at the Bush School in Seattle, Washington. She has also been a district K–12 reading/language arts coordinator and classroom teacher. Her research interests include children's literature, comprehension, and response to literature. She has been on the authorship team of Macmillan/McGraw Hill's K–8 New View reading texts and A New View language arts texts, and she also has been a contributing author on professional books about multicultural literature. Recently Aoki was appointed by the governor to Washington State's Professional Educator Standards Board. She has won numerous educational awards including Washington State's Award for Excellence in Education and University of Washington's Distinguished Graduate Award. She lives in Seattle with her husband and three-year-old daughter.

Ruth Nathan, one of the authors of *Writers Express* and *Write Away,* is the author of many professional books and articles on literacy. She earned a Ph.D. in reading from Oakland University in Rochester, Michigan, where she co-headed their reading research laboratory for several years. She currently teaches third grade as well as consults with numerous schools and organizations on reading.

Karen Patricia Smith is professor at the Queens College Graduate School of Library and Information Studies in Flushing, New York, where she teaches courses in school library media, children's literature, and research methods. She has published numerous articles and reviews in *Journal of Youth Services in Libraries, School Library Journal, Bookbird,* and *The ALAN Review.* She is author of *The Fabulous Realm: A Literary–Historical Approach to British Fantasy, 1780– 1990* (1993) and editor of *African-American Voices in*

Young Adult Literature: Tradition, Transition, Transformation (1994). She also served as editor for the *Library Trends* (Winter, 1993) issue titled "Multicultural Children's Literature in the United States," and the *Library Trends* (Spring, 1996) issue titled "Imagination and Scholarship: The Contributions of Women to American Children's and Young Adult Literature and Services." Smith has co-authored the column Connecting Educators with Professional Resources with Myra Zarnowski for *The New Advocate*. Additionally, she has served as a member of the Board of Directors of the Children's Literature Association and is currently co-chair of the Orbis Pictus Award Committee of the National Council of Teachers of English. Smith has given numerous presentations on children's literature and young adult literature within the United States and in Australia, Spain, and Sweden.

Contributors

Rhoda Blumberg cannot remember a time when she was not attracted to stories, especially the true stories from history. Her writing reveals a fascination with travel and exploration, two processes that replace legendary stories and speculation with living fact. Her work also demonstrates sensitivity to the perspectives of native peoples encountered by travelers and explorers. Her focus on accurate detail results in books that stand out because of their judicious use of endnotes and grounding in primary and authoritative secondary sources. Readers remember Blumberg's 1985 Newbery honor book, *Commodore Perry in the Land of the Shogun*. Since then, the 1990 and 1997 Orbis Pictus Award Committees have bestowed honors on *The Great American Gold Rush* and *Full Steam Ahead: The Race to Build a Transcontinental Railroad*, respectively.

Jennifer Owings Dewey grew up in the rural West of the 1950s, surrounded by all the natural world has to offer. Equally important influences in her life were her father, Nathaniel Owings, who designed the first land-use plan to protect the scenic Big Sur coast, and her stepmother, Margaret Wentworth Owings, a tireless defender of the wilderness and advocate for sea otters and mountain lions. It is not surprising that Dewey's writing and illustrating combine a fascination with wildlife and a respect for its place in the environment. This interest has taken her as far as Antarctica. Dewey is the author of *Wildlife Rescue: The Work of Dr. Kathleen Ramsey*, a 1995 Orbis Pictus honor book. She received the Scientific American Young Readers Book Award for *Mud Matters: Stories from a Mud Lover*. Recently, she recounted her Antarctic adventures in *Antarctic Journal: Four Months at the Bottom of the World*.

Jean Fritz has always been fascinated by what it means to be American, perhaps because she is a U.S. citizen raised in China during her early years. This preoccupation is evident in her biographical writing for children. Her "question biographies," labeled for the nature of their titles, focus on historical standouts such as Paul Revere, Samuel Adams, John Hancock, Benjamin Franklin, Patrick Henry, and King George III. Fritz has commented that figures seem to leap out of the past and demand that she tell their stories. That is when the research begins, a task she deeply loves. For Fritz, research often means traveling to sites where the person walked and breathed so she can know her subject intimately. Honing a style that uses humor and humanizing detail to draw readers into history, Fritz's writing has earned awards and honors for more than thirty years. In 1990 her biography *The Great Little Madison* earned the inaugural Orbis Pictus Award. Four years earlier, the American Library Association gave her the Laura Ingalls Wilder Award for her enduring contribution to children's literature.

James Cross Giblin wrote for the student newspaper in high school and acted in school plays. These interests led him to major in English and dramatic arts in college. Three years after graduation, he began a career in publishing and five years later entered the children's market as an associate editor at Lothrop, Lee and Shepard Books. After five years, he moved to Seabury Press, becoming editor in chief. Still interested in writing, he contributed to *The Horn Book Magazine* and *Cricket*, a magazine for children. Readers recognize Giblin as the author of nonfiction books with unusual historical subjects, such as *From Hand to Mouth: Or, How We Invented Knives, Forks, Spoons, and Chopsticks and the Table Manners to Go with Them.* For two of his biographical works, *Charles A. Lindbergh: A Human Hero* and *The Amazing Life of Benjamin Franklin,* he received Orbis Pictus honors, in 1998 and 2001 respectively.

Patricia Lauber has for years enjoyed standing and staring at the world, talking to people, and reading a lot. All of these processes have fed her childhood desire to write. And for almost fifty years she has done just that. Her nonfiction has taken readers on journeys through the universe, providing microscopic and telescopic views of subjects such as forest fires, backyard flowers, fossilized animal remains, and geologic formations on other planets. Lauber is the author of the 1987 Newbery honor book *Volcano: The Eruption and Healing of Mount St. Helens.* She also is recognized for *The News about Dinosaurs,* a 1990 Orbis Pictus honor book, and *Seeing Earth from Space,* a 1991 Orbis Pictus honor book. Her book *Hurricanes: Earth's Mightiest Storms* appeared on the Orbis Pictus Award Committee's recommended list.

Jim Murphy grew up in Kearny, New Jersey, graduated from Rutgers University, and became a nationally ranked track athlete. He and his friends often hopped on trains to explore Newark and New York City where he loved to watch people. Following a stint as a construction worker, Jim landed a job with Seabury Press. Over a seven-year period, he moved from editorial secretary to managing editor. But as he noticed that the authors with whom he worked were receiving great reviews and decent royalty checks, he decided to pursue a writer's life. Few nonfiction writers have received the accolades that Murphy has. Part of his success rests on a long-standing fascination with eyewitness accounts. Capturing voices and images from the past to illuminate his texts, Murphy's work has earned two Golden Kite Awards, for *The Boy's War: Confederate and Union Soldiers Talk about the Civil War* in 1990 and *The Long Road to Gettysburg* in 1992. It also has netted him two Orbis Pictus Awards, the first in 1994 for *Across America on an Emigrant Train* and the second in 1996 for *The Great Fire,* which also was a Newbery honor book. In addition, his book *Blizzard! The Storm That Changed America* received a Sibert honor in 2001.

Mary Pope Osborne was the child of a military man and consequently moved frequently. In college she became fascinated with world mythology and comparative religion, ultimately becoming a religion major. After graduating from the University of North Carolina at Chapel Hill, she traveled the world, camping in a cave on Crete and surviving an earthquake in northern Afghanistan, a riot in Kabul, and blood poisoning in Kathmandu, Nepal. All of these experiences have contributed to her writing for children. Although Osborne is best known for her fiction, she received a 1997 Orbis Pictus honor for *One World, Many Religions: The Ways We Worship.* A joint committee of the Children's Book Council and the National Council for the Social Studies named this book a Notable Trade Book in the Field of Social Studies.

Laurence Pringle immersed himself in nature as a child. He watched birds, studied flowers, and observed all sorts of wildlife in natural settings. He was a hunter, a fisher, and a trapper. As he matured, Pringle studied wildlife biology, developing an interest in the impact of humans on the natural world. In 1978 he received a special award from the National Wildlife Federation in recognition of his commitment to conservation. His books, which draw children's attention to their kinship with other living creatures, are an outgrowth of these experiences. Pringle is the author of *An Extraordinary Life: The Story of a Monarch Butterfly,* winner of the 1998 Orbis Pictus Award, and *Dolphin Man: Exploring the World of Dolphins,* a 1996 Orbis Pictus honor book. He also is known for his contributions to *Audubon, Ranger Rick, Highlights for Children,* and *Smithsonian.*

Diane Swanson explored the natural setting of Lethridge, Alberta, Canada, as a child. She took long summer walks to the lake with her terrier and poked around her yard, looking for ladybugs and spiders. Today, life is not much different. Instead of walking to the lake, she walks along the sea near her home in Victoria, British Columbia, exploring the wondrous outdoors. These experiences have directly fed her writing. In fact, her first article for the nature magazine *Ranger Rick* dealt with ladybugs, and her first book, *Toothy Tongue and One Long Foot,* focused on nature activities in her backyard. The 1995 Orbis Pictus Award Committee bestowed their award on Swanson's book *Safari beneath the Sea: The Wonder World of the North Pacific Coast.* In the United States, readers also will discover her other science books, including *Buffalo Sunrise: The Story of a North American Giant, Animals Eat the Weirdest Things,* and her contributions to the Up Close series.

This book was typeset in Avant Garde and Palatino by Electronic Imaging.
Typefaces used on the cover are Carolina and Garamond Narrow.
This book was printed on 60-lb. Williamsburg Offset paper by Versa Press.